Against
the Wind

Against the Wind

Pedalling for a **pint** from
Japan to **Ireland**

YASUYUKI OZEKI

Translated by Robert Heffill

POOLBEG

Published 2004 by Poolbeg Press Ltd.
123 Grange Hill, Baldoyle,
Dublin 13, Ireland
Email: poolbeg@poolbeg.com

1 3 5 7 9 10 8 6 4 2

A catalogue record for this book is available from the British Library

ISBN 1-84223-209-6

Typeset by Patricia Hope in Sabon MT 11.5/15.5
Printed by
CPD Group, Wales

www.poolbeg.com

About the author

Having decided to hop off the 'escalator of life' in Japan, Yasuyuki Ozeki completed a mammoth personal cycling challenge – from Japan to Ireland. He turned his extraordinary journey into a book, *Against the Wind,* which was first published in Japan in 2002. This autumn, Yaz will tackle his '7 Peaks in 7 Weeks' project – a cycling tour around Ireland which will include the assent of each of its highest peaks, with his bike on his back.

Unable to resist the call of a good pint of the black stuff, Yaz is planning a permanent move to Ireland.

Acknowledgements

Special thanks to Mr Colm Conyngham of Bridgestone, Ireland for his everlasting support for my projects, to Robert – my translator – for his great effort and output on this job, to Masha and Pecha for the Russian spelling check, to all Poolbeg staff especially Kieran, Paula and Anne for their encouragement and a great job, and to my fiancée, Fiona, for her support with this book and in my messy life.

To my grandmother, Haruyo,
for me the very best Japanese person

Contents

Prologue

My first experience of Ireland

*Christy Moore *Fairytale of New York*
CHRISTY MOORE LIVE AT THE POINT

Othello House, Lower Gardiner St., Dublin.
Christmas Eve, 1994

"What in the name of God are you thinking, Yazel?"

Frank, the clerk working at the B&B, had called me 'Yazel'. He had been on reception when I first visited in March of that year. At check-in, I had told him that 'Yasu' was easier to say than 'Yasuyuki'. Frank proceeded to enter Yazel in the guest book in bold letters, informing me, with a grin, that this was now my name.

"Hardly anywhere will be open, not even restaurants. Seeing as tomorrow is Christmas Day, just about everywhere is going to be closed – department stores, supermarkets, restaurants, newsagents, everywhere. The trains and buses won't be running either. Everything will be shut. I'll be the only person you'll find working."

Frank, white-haired with thick milk-bottle-bottom glasses,

---

* 'I made out a list of songs to inspire me as I cycled along my journey. Each day I would choose one and sing it for that day.

proffered this advice, along with a strong smell of cigarettes and Guinness.

"But we're talking about the Irish, so one or two pubs should be open, right?"

I was looking forward to chatting with the locals who would be drinking in the pub, even on Christmas Day. Even if there were nothing to eat, a good Guinness would have been feast enough. "What are you like, Yazel? Even the barmen are on holiday tomorrow. It's a holy day for God's sake." Not worrying about it, nor knowing quite what I was going to do the next day, I went to return to my room when Frank's voice boomed out, "No problem, Yazel! No problem. It'll be fine tomorrow. I've a feeling that things will work out for you!"

At about three o'clock the following afternoon, I stood on a rocky promontory at Sandycove, gazing at the rough sea. Just as Frank had said, Dublin was silent on Christmas Day. Nowhere was open; the city was in a state of suspended animation. There was nothing else to do except walk, so I had decided to head for Sandycove, famous for its Joyce Tower. There I could see the sea, described by James Joyce in *Ulysses* as the 'snot green sea'. I love this sea, a sad, tempestuous sea. I just wanted to gaze on it for a while.

When I got there I beheld a peculiar scene. People had come along in twos and threes, undressed down to their swimsuits and were now plunging into the freezing sea where they swam around screaming. Crusty old men, flabby middle-aged men, even dogs! A small bottle of whiskey nestled in the hand of one girl who stood with a worried face staring at her boyfriend in the water. I went over after he had scuttled up the rocks, trembling with cold and as he drank some whiskey to get warm I asked why they were doing this. "They say that if you jump into the sea here on Christmas Day, then it'll bring you luck for the coming year. It's a Christmas tradition."

They shared some of their whiskey with me. I suppose it would have tasted even better if I'd taken the plunge. I felt the water and it was absolutely freezing. Something was amiss here. People who could do this were different. They were mad. Whilst I envied them, there was no way I could do something like that.

To my dismay, a man came up, put an arm firmly around my shoulders and asked, "Do you want to give it a try?" No way. It would be great if I had been strong enough to, but I simply couldn't bear the thought. It was out of the question.

"Well, never mind. Anyway, if you come along I'll explain how these guys can do this sort of thing." The middle-aged man, who had a face like Frank Sinatra and the toned body of a rugby player, led me off. Opening a gate to a big house, which faced the sea, we entered, then passed through another door. We were inside his house. After a warm greeting from his wife, I was taken upstairs. "Hang on a moment," said sportsman Sinatra going back downstairs. I wondered why on earth I had been brought up here, when all I wanted to know was why they swam out there in the middle of winter! The door opened and there stood Sinatra in a swimsuit. He tossed over a blue swimsuit and a bath towel, exclaiming, "It's simple. You'll find out when you jump in." I was overwhelmed and Sinatra, catching me off-guard whispered into my ear, "If you jump in, you'll be able to tell your grandchildren all about it. That on Christmas Day in 1994, you jumped into the Irish Sea beside the Joyce Tower."

The word 'grandchildren' convinced me. This word alone transformed swimming in the middle of winter. I now saw a fairytale. Sinatra leapt from his garden into the sea shouting "Come on, come on!" Spurred on by his voice, I plunged full tilt into the water. In that moment and without flinching, I resigned myself to dying.

I crashed through the waves and into the sea . . . the sparkling winter sea . . . that clear, emerald green . . . Irish green. This inspiring thought was superseded instantly by the icy coldness shooting through my body. I was dying! I had to grab the ladder and get out fast . . . .When I came to my senses, I noticed Sinatra was with me and that we were both leaping around waving both hands in the air to keep warm. What the heck was I doing?

The next thing I knew I was sipping whiskey beside a hearth with a wood fire.

"Well done, son, well done. A samurai, that's what you are. By the way, will you be going along to any Christmas parties tonight?" asked Sinatra.

Of course not, even McDonald's would probably be out of the question today.

"Right. You're to be with us then. How about cutting up the turkey? We can't have you dining on a Big Mac on Christmas Eve. Forget that."

The next moment I was dishing up the turkey on plates for Gene (Sinatra), Ohna (his wife) and a couple who were neighbourhood friends. From a broad, tall window in the dining room we could see the night scene across Dublin Bay. The long threads of Christmas lights looked so beautiful. I had been resigned to missing dinner that night, so all this seemed like a dream. Not five minutes into the meal, Gene suddenly asked me, "What's your ambition?" I was surprised by the abruptness of the question, but I recounted my dream, my 'ambition' to them. It had come to me like a flash of lightning in September that year and I had been unable to forget it.

"I fell in love with Ireland when I first arrived here in March. And it wasn't just the Guinness. It was the people, their kindness, their smiling faces and the unhurried, gentle pace of life here. The gap, the distance between here and Japan and me felt unbelievably vast. The Eurasian continent lies between the two countries. What would it be like to cross Eurasia by bicycle, under my own steam, all the way to Ireland? And what lies between Ireland and Japan? What did that distance, that gap signify? I wanted to discover some of the answers to these questions as I pedalled. I wanted to kick down the distance." Gene had been gazing out at the night scene, quietly listening. When I finished talking, he turned to me, tears in his eyes.

"Fantastic, a really fine story. Thanks, Yasu. You have to do it. You just have to."

In that moment I knew that there would be no going back. I couldn't betray this man and his tears. Christmas night, 1994. My epic journey began at the Joyce Tower. I became a pedalling Bloom.

Why Ireland? Why Eurasia? Why by bicycle?

Even though I had gone to a University of Foreign Studies, I hadn't been abroad until the time of my graduation trip. This was not intentional. I always wanted to, but the four years slipped quickly by and I simply didn't get round to it. Whilst the students around me got excited and headed for the four corners, my days and nights were taken up with part-time jobs, girls and reading. I had somehow persuaded myself not to follow the herd. After all what were they doing going abroad when they didn't even know Japan? Nearing completion of my graduation thesis, my professor tried encouraging me. "Why don't you go to Peru, seeing as you are writing about the history of the Andes?" I did think how nice it would be to go abroad at least once before I found a job, although to be honest, Latin America was not really somewhere that appealed to me. This was possibly because many of my fellow students were heading off in that direction and I simply wanted to go somewhere else, to a place no-one had told me about. This finally persuaded me that it had to be Ireland. There was nothing particularly special about the country. Down-to-earth, emotional people . . . Tasty beverages . . . Pub music . . .

A month in Ireland turned out to be a hugely important episode for me. There was life in the faces of everyone I passed on the streets. At that time in 1994 it was by no means an affluent country. There was laughter and joy everywhere. Eyes twinkled. The very fact of having had to overcome adversity seemed to give the people a frankness and warmth that made you feel they understood the suffering of others. These folk were naturally generous with others. They possessed the inner strength to live in the present, rather than living in the past or being afraid of what the future might hold. There was the unhurried passage of time. Complementing these characteristics, or perhaps symbolic of them all, were the music, the dance, the talks on literature and nights in the pub. I came to Ireland expecting nothing, but found so much. Back in Japan I cried when I remembered the people I had met in Ireland, the laughter, the hands outstretched in warm greetings, the toasts we had exchanged.

I felt an unbridgeable gap between Japan, where I now stood, and Ireland.

Before I got to know Ireland, and when I began looking for a job, the state of Japanese society, the way people lived and a host of other issues had plagued my mind. From those hazy notions grew the conviction that 'I had to do something'. Doing something was all well and fine but it just wasn't clear exactly what it was I should do. I was confronted by a number of doors in Japan. Had I opened one of them and tumbled into the world beyond and so at least started out in some direction, it would have been fine. Not knowing which door I should choose, or what lay beyond the doors, I ended up stuck in limbo, going round in circles in a virtual vestibule. In situations like this, I imagine everyone feels the need to resolve the crisis, or frustration at their inability to work it out. I was very acutely aware of these feelings. This was the state of things when I travelled to Ireland. On returning to Japan, I found myself bewildered by the unbridgeable gap between the two countries. On top of that I felt unable to do anything decisive about the situation. The days turned into months, then one night at a local beach, just when I felt I couldn't take any more, what felt like a chemical reaction rocked my head and my heart. It happened in a flash.

'To Ireland, across Eurasia, by bicycle.'

The idea struck me like a thunderbolt from the blue. Then it was gone.

The gap between Ireland and Japan between Ireland and me . . . the gap filled by the Eurasian continent, this was the gap that I would have to cross. The Eurasian continent and Ireland that lay beyond it seemed like a distant stage on the far side of a door at the top of a flight of stairs. Most people would probably say that going to Ireland and living there would only be another temporary step in life. But as far as I was concerned, such a stage was necessary. At least it was an unambiguous, real stage.

So, why did it have to be by bike? Planes, vehicles, trains, motorbikes – weren't there any number of ways I could go? The answer was clear and simple. Since I had felt the gap and it had grown in my mind, I was determined to bridge it under my own steam. I had to kick down the distance with my own two feet. Walking was an option, but I would probably have spent the rest of my life doing it. When I thought about the moderate speed and the wind rushing past my body, lifting my soul, I concluded that by bicycle was the only way to go. There will doubtless be those who still wonder exactly what led me to do this. I can offer no further explanation, except to add just one comment. Surely even Lindbergh, the man who dared to attempt the first solo flight across the Atlantic Ocean, must, one day somewhere out in the middle of a prairie, have been hit by a thunderbolt from the blue?

1

Preliminary preparations and the quest of a dream

In my 'Child's First Years' book it says 'Hasn't settled down since the moment he started walking. He's a child who likes to head off by himself', and 'He loves his bike and goes off riding around the neighbourhood'. So perhaps I was just born like that. Not being a fanatic, though, I didn't learn much about repairing bikes, nor did I gain any real cycling experience. What I had said to Gene might have seemed outrageous, but all I knew was that Ireland lay on the other side of the globe and in between lay the vast Eurasian continent. How far was it and how long would it take for heaven's sake? Which countries would I pass through? Given that there were, most likely, countries you couldn't cross, might I ultimately be prevented from cycling across Eurasia anyway? Where and how would I sleep? What would I eat? Ireland, my goal, glittered enticingly and I was oblivious to anything else. As far as I was concerned, Eurasia was totally unknown territory. I was determined to give cycling a chance anyway. So I got out the mountain bike I had used for a year whilst I was at university and then put aside, and started cycling around the local area on days off work. My home was in the city of Suita and my cycling range was soon from central Suita to central Osaka, a distance of some 10 km. In due course I was able to push it as far as Kobe, a further 30km. I discovered I could really go places. I began to realise the potential of bicycles. I pedalled a certain distance every day and if I managed to cycle without stopping before the end, I entertained the notion that I might just be able to cross the continent and make it as far as Ireland.

So then I thought I would try cycling with some baggage mounted on the bike. I just carried the bare essentials – a change of clothing, a sleeping bag and a sleeping mat – and took the ferry to Tokushima. From Tokushima I would cycle to Kochi, Matsuyama, Hiroshima, Okayama, Kobe and on to Osaka. Once I'd made up my mind, I did the route in five days, without a tent. I slept rough. However, it became clear that I needed a tent for safety and for shelter from the rain. So I bought a tent, loaded it with the rest of my gear and set out on my next journey . . .

For the next three and a half years I continued my preparation and built up my strength in advance of my departure. However drunk I got at parties, I would do a 20km local cycle ride every night. I avoided using cars (I actually sold my beloved VW Golf), trains, and buses and switched to travelling by bike. When the prospect arose at work of being transferred to Tokyo, I decided to leave. This is effectively where I stepped off the 'escalator of life', but as I had a clear target in mind, I was not worried about taking the step. I toughened up over the next year and a half or so, working on a building site.

* * *

My next goal was to try getting to the peak of Mount Fuji by bike. If I couldn't do this, Eurasia was out of the question. This strange notion gripped me and I trained that year from spring through into the summer. I did a waterfall walk on Mount Mino with my bicycle strapped to my rucksack. After that I climbed Mount Mino, Mount Ibuki (in the rain), and Mount Fuji. Cycling from the first to the fifth station on Fuji, I shouldered the bike to the top from there. Well, at least I got to the top and now I began to feel that I would be strong enough for the Eurasia trip.

So, when, which way, and how was I going to get to Ireland? I bought several books on bicycle journeys. The Silk Road route across Eurasia had been cycled, through China, Iran, Iraq and Turkey. The route across China, Kazakhstan, the Ukraine and Europe did not appear to have been done by anyone, so I thought I would buy the relevant travel guides and maps. I did my own research and used the Internet. All the information suggested that this route was too risky. There were too many huge distances to cover between towns and there would be difficulty in obtaining food and water in the wide desert regions of Kazakhstan. I spent several months researching a route. At about that time I read an article in a newspaper entitled 'Crossing Siberia by Bicycle'. I hadn't considered the possibility of crossing Russia by bike via the Mongolia-Siberia route. I had dreamed about going to Mongolia for years, so I decided that it had to be this route.

Promotion tour to Ireland

If only there were a few people prepared to welcome me when I eventually got to Ireland after my long cycle journey from Japan. I flew to Ireland in Spring 1997 with this thought in my mind. I was intent on talking about my plans to anyone willing to listen, whether in the pubs or in the media. Would any of them meet me when I eventually arrived safely? If they did, then the cycling would have been worth it. My destination and those waiting there for me, would be a greater incentive.

I had sent out documents, including my travel plans, to the media, as well as to companies such as Guinness, but having received no replies (unsurprisingly) by the time of my departure I decided that I would set out on foot and knock on doors when I arrived in Dublin. My first stop was the National Tourist Office. There I talked to Leo Ganter, who was responsible for Asia. He gave me some ideas of how to go about getting visas for each country and introduced me to Liam Campbell, who was responsible for cycling in Ireland. The next day I spoke to Liam, who suggested that if I wrote a detailed plan, the Irish Tourist Board might be able to provide me with a letter of introduction and with that I might be able to get visas for the different countries.

Next I handed over my travel plans to a lady on reception at the *Irish Times* newspaper. She told me that the relevant person might contact me. When I visited the *Evening Herald* newspaper a young journalist, Niamh Hooper, promptly invited me along to the canteen and interviewed me in some depth. The next day I spoke to Tony from the sports desk at RTE. He listened to what I had to say and asked me to send him a copy of my detailed plan when it was ready. I dropped into the RTE Radio Centre also and had a chat with Colin Morrison, a producer. Apparently, 2FM's Gerry Ryan Show dealt with this kind of 'unusual' project, so he told me he would put it to producer Paul Russell. My travel plan was copied and bound in the broadcasting office and the friendly lady on reception passed it on to Paul Russell.

A message from Paul Russell was waiting for me when I got back to my lodgings. He wanted to meet me the next day. I went back to the *Irish Times* and asked the receptionist how my proposal had been received. I was taken along to meet the journalist responsible for special interest stories (News Features), Alva MacSherry. She said she had been waiting for me. I had an extensive interview with her that lasted about an hour. I headed back to RTE and met Paul Russell in the Gerry Ryan Show staff room, as well as Gerry Ryan himself. I would be on the programme, on the phone, on Monday morning, so I was asked to think hard over the weekend about what I would say. They were going to follow my progress on the programme, and hey, they wanted me to come into the studio to talk when I arrived in Dublin!

On the following Monday morning I phoned in to the Gerry Ryan Show and told the listeners what my plans and aspirations were. Gerry gave me great encouragement. and urged his listeners to come forward as sponsors. It had been an intense week. It felt like a dream. I hadn't expected things to turn out like this. Gazing out of the aeroplane window at the green earth below I thought to myself 'no way I'd have got this far in any other country'. Two national newspapers carried articles about my project in the days that followed. I got back to Japan and, suffering jetlag, I was having a nap when the telephone rang. On the phone I heard a man speaking English from somewhere far away: "This is Colm Conyngham of Bridgestone Ireland here. You know Bridgestone, the Japanese tyre manufacturer? That Bridgestone."

My eyes popped open and I sat bolt upright. "I heard the Gerry Ryan Show the other day. We may be able to provide sponsorship, although what form it might take is not clear yet . . . maybe a Bridgestone bicycle or financial backing." My eyes opened wider still, draining my right nostril that had been blocked with hay fever. "Could you send us a detailed plan by October? There is a meeting then about budgets for the next financial year."

I was dumbstruck. For several hours, no, days after the call I was in a daze. I was naturally happy about the bicycle and the money, but the thing that pleased me most was that there was a company in Ireland prepared to make such an offer. I imagined that having a formal sponsor would make it much easier to obtain visas. That alone would be sufficient. I was supposed to submit a plan by October. If I could find a sponsor, it would automatically mean starting the trip the following spring. I had to speed up my preparations.

From Beijing I would cross the Gobi Desert to Ulan Bator. From there onward to Lake Baikal and westward across Siberia to Moscow. Then northwest via Saint Petersburg, Helsinki, Stockholm and Denmark, to Germany . . . Unfolding the map, I divided up the route into days of about 100 kilometres. If I reckoned on one day of rest for every five days of cycling, it appeared I could reach Dublin in about five and a half months. I did a rough calculation of how much my daily food and living expenses would be in each country. Apart from in the larger towns, I would camp. I wanted to keep my accommodation expenses to a minimum. Then there was the cost of buying the additional equipment. Adding all these up gave me a budget. A sponsor would make their decision based on this plan, so it had to be quite detailed.

When should I set out? Mongolia and Siberia were a problem. If I left early in the year I might freeze to death. If I left it too late, Mongolia would be too hot and insects would outnumber the stars in Siberia. After consulting some useful guidebooks that described the weather, as well as other sources of information, I decided I would leave at the end of March. It took about three to four months to put together the detailed plan. I submitted it to Bridgestone Ireland in August. It would certainly prove useful material for my visa applications, even if I couldn't find a sponsor.

In October I had another call from Colm Conyngham, Marketing Manager at Bridgestone Ireland. "I've some great news for you." Bridgestone Ireland was prepared to be an official sponsor. This would mean back-up for my visa applications for each country, a bike, financial support and maybe even help with accommodation in various countries in Europe. I heard the words as if in a dream, and collapsed onto the tatami mats.

"Really!?"

A Russian visa

The greatest obstacle during my preparations and indeed the key to getting things started was obtaining a Russian visa. This was to prove even more difficult than the journey itself. For about a year, I used every means at my disposal and every connection I had to try and get a visa, without success. I visited the Russian consulate in Osaka with my Russian friend, Pecha, and met the vice-consul. Who would be responsible if something were to happen to me? I would not get permission if a sponsor could not provide overall support, rather than merely financial backing, particularly in view of the fact that I was not just cycling, but cycling alone. Bridgestone's Colm Conyngham went along to the Russian Embassy in Dublin to request a visa on my behalf, to have his request denied and be told, in no uncertain terms, that "Crime is rife in Russia. What would happen if he were to die? We certainly don't want to be responsible." I learned later that it was at this point that the seriousness of his responsibilities in this project dawned on Colm. Wherever I turned, I found that people were simply not prepared to take any responsibility for a cyclist travelling alone.

I visited the Tokyo Head Office of Bridgestone to sort out a letter of introduction from Bridgestone's Moscow office. Everyone there was most kind and showed warm interest in my plans, but they were wary when it came to the issue of visas. They too had misgivings about being able to take any responsibility were something to happen to me. Two months passed without any progress. It was now three weeks before my intended day of departure and I was at my wits' end. I had knocked on all possible doors. Not being able to cross Russia, I would be forced to alter my route at the last moment. I decided to use my last trump card, my friend Teppei. I had read about Teppei in a newspaper when he crossed Siberia by bike. I beseeched him to use whatever contacts he had and although it eventually meant paying through the nose, he obtained a Russian visa in the twinkling of an eye. There were conditions attached to the visa however. The period of the visa was from May 21st to the end of July. I would not be allowed in before that date or to leave any later. Were there to be any changes, these would entail time and money wherever I was at the time. My route was specified too. The larger towns I would have to pass through were nearly all noted on the visa and I was not to deviate from this course. My passage and accommodation in the legs between the towns were described as 'In transit'. This was typical of Russia. However, given that in the not-too-distant past it would have been unthinkable for a foreigner to drift around Russia on a bike, I had to appreciate how liberal Russia had become.

* * *

Warren and Yasue

Warren has sideburns like Elvis. An Australian who moved to Britain, he worked as an English conversation teacher in my Japanese company. After class, we would have a drink together in a pub or bar and in due course became good friends. He was working as an English teacher only temporarily. He worked privately as an 'artist' creating original designs and surreal pictures. One evening in a bar, downing pints, we got on to the subject of helmets. If I wore a helmet, it couldn't be a bog-standard helmet. Warren would design it. What about having a Eurasian continent painted on the helmet with the Japanese flag on the back, and the Irish tricolour on the front? If I had the main towns along the way on it, I could extend the line along the route as I reached each of them. That way I could explain to anyone I couldn't communicate with along the way where I'd come from and where I was going, just by lowering my head. During my visit to Ireland in the winter of 1995, I searched for a helmet that was big enough to draw the map on. If I could, I wanted to buy a helmet in Ireland, and to use it as a canvas to be painted with Eurasia and the route I would pedal. I found the ideal helmet in a cycle shop, Hardings, on the banks of the

Liffey. It was second-hand, but better than the new ones. I asked Peter, the owner, how much it cost. "Don't worry about that. I hope it brings you good luck on your journey." Warren then spent many months working on the helmet. The continents were painted in, and a knife used to etch relief onto the surface. After the application of numerous layers of lacquer, the helmet was transformed into a true work of art. It was unique, and probably the first of its type in the history of the world! One evening, snacking on green soybeans in a bar, Warren came up with another idea. What would I do about gear? I couldn't just wear boring cycling gear. He said he would design it, and his wife Yasue would make the outfit. The cycling top, which took a considerable amount of time and money to produce, was a vivid green and had a cool design with the word Dinamo printed across the chest. Dinamo is the name of the 'Dreamers Club', a club set up by Warren, myself and some other friends. Warren is the club manager. I had no idea how many members belonged to this particular club, but there would be at least one 'dreamer' pedalling around wearing this top.

Bicycle and equipment preparations (see appendix on page 241)

Bridgestone did not manufacture or sell bicycles in Europe, so an order was sent through to Bridgestone cycles, through Bridgestone head office, for a mountain bike. The tailor-made Bridgestone bike was the colour of the Irish tricolour. From the top down, it was green, white, and orange. Warren christened it Rocket Boy ONE.

As far as possible I decided to avoid taking any unnecessary items and those I would take would need to be as light and small as possible. However, in view of the great distance I was planning to cycle, I would be unable to carry all my equipment. I decided to forward baggage to three places along the way; Irkutsk, Novosibirsk and Chelyabinsk. This included tyres and freeze-dried foods. It appeared that Russian post offices would look after items for one month, so I calculated the dates when I would arrive and gave a list with instructions on what to post and when to my mum.

* * *

Deciding on a detailed schedule

A junior student introduced me to her friend, Shibano, who was studying in Mongolia. I called Shibano in Ulan Bator and she offered the following advice. Firstly spring starts in about mid-May in Mongolia and sandstorms sweep the Mongolian steppes during April. She had read about incidents where children of nomads had been literally blown away and killed by the winds. Apparently things improved from the end of May. Taking into consideration both this information and the timing of my arrival in Siberia, I decided on setting out on the 16th April (even though it would still only be very early spring in Mongolia), in order to see the famous green grass of Mongolia.

Language problems

How far could I get in areas where I could not communicate? To be honest, I wanted to experience what it was like being in that sort of situation, so I resolved not to do any language study. Apart from in China, where I would be able to communicate by writing, I would need to rely entirely on body language.

I paid a visit to Ms Egan at the Irish Embassy before

leaving, hardly expecting it to amount to anything more than a simple gesture of friendship between Japan and Ireland. She received me with overwhelming warmth and kindness and asked if I could take a pile of three-leaf clover shamrock stickers with me on the road, to promote the country. She also gave me a list of addresses of Irish embassies on my route and the names of senior officials at the embassies. She said she would contact them in advance to let them know I was coming. She also introduced me to Conor O'Clery, *Irish Times* correspondent in Beijing.

Sponsors are not sponsors for nothing. Bridgestone Ireland would, of course, want some publicity in return. Having said that, I didn't do much PR at all. Colm prepared a pre-departure press release and all I had to do was check it. Bridgestone had offices in each country I would travel through in Europe and Colm would let them know in advance that I was coming. He was also working hard in discussions with the Gerry Ryan Show. I appeared on the programme a week before my departure. My job was just to cycle safely and report in to the programme on the way. Gerry boosted my morale and gave me huge encouragement. "There won't be any creamy Guinness out there in the middle of the Gobi Desert you know, but the best of luck anyway!"

A message from U2

In March, with my departure imminent, U2 came on tour to Japan. So just before my trip to Ireland, I got to see them on stage. I gave Warren and Yasue tickets as a present to thank them for the work they had done for me up to then.

Warren did something really kind for me in secret. He got in touch with Paul Russell, producer on the Gerry Ryan

Show, asking if he could arrange for me to meet the members of U2 when they came to Osaka. Their schedule was too busy but they did send me a wonderful message of encouragement which said, 'A Big good luck from the band!' This message and the performance on stage reinforced my resolve to succeed in my Eurasian journey.

Finally I did a fully loaded dress-rehearsal trip on my new bike to Kyushu. My family, various relatives, friends and junior students also planned special dinners for me. I ate and drank loads every evening. It felt as if I was stocking myself up as you would a larder in preparation for the rigours of the journey ahead.

The next moment I was on the ferry 'Yan Jing' from Kobe bound for Tianjin in China. At the other end of the streamers was my older sister. My friends were there too, waving wildly under a clear sky.

There was no turning back now.

The boat was heading for Tianjin.

2

April 18th 2:35pm

U2 – *Where The Streets Have No Name*
THE JOSHUA TREE

Right foot down . . . first push of the pedal . . . left foot down
. . . the second push . . . three, four, five, six, seven . . .

How many times would the pedals turn between here and
Dublin? Such thoughts made my head swim and although I
couldn't help but have them, if I was going to end up lost and
bewildered, then it would be better to turn back immediately.

There was really nothing for it but to go with the flow,
further!

A beaten up old minibus with people I had met on the
ferry kindly went ahead to show me the way. The vehicle
occupants included my new friend, Watatsune, there on a
study trip from Nankai University and with whom I was to
stay that night, and Ganbator, a Mongolian I had promised
to meet up with again in Ulan Bator. Tianjin is a region
famous in China for its manufacturing industry. The air
quality is quite poor. Hard ash, drifting like clouds of lead
pencil shavings, got stuck in my mouth and throat. Was it

coal they were burning? Photochemical smog, or whatever it was, left my eyes stinging. On top of that, I had to look out for potholes as I cycled along the road. Concentrating on the road, I lost sight of the bus, seemed to take a wrong turning and before I knew it was travelling along a motorway. (I was told later that the bus had tried to stop for me, but I had missed them and sailed past.) A great start!

I was not going back. I didn't want to. I had to accept that I could and would take wrong roads. The motorway was straight and provided a shortcut. Or so I told myself as I pressed on. Cars, trucks, buses, motorcycles, they all piled past me honking their horns. I could see people smiling. Some were waving. They seemed to be welcoming me, supporting me. This wasn't a time for such optimistic speculation. Perhaps they were all really mad at me? The smiling faces were probably just winding me up.

These thoughts began to stir a sense of panic, so I exited the motorway at a sign that said 'Public Road'. As I suspected, the 'public road' turned out to be a normal road. It was narrow, but trucks and bicycles still thundered by, both laden with vegetables. Residents and traders along the road stared in curiosity at me. Many of them pointed at me and laughed. This was my first experience of feeling like a traveller, an odd stranger on a bike loaded with red bags. All sorts of shops lined the road, selling vegetables, meat, fruit, straw hats, frying pans and buns. It was like an endless pageant passing by. I was overwhelmed and surprised by it all. Avoiding glances, I bowled on and in no time I found myself at Tianjin station. Tall rows of buildings had been built in the centre of what I now realised was a really huge city. Watatsune was waiting as arranged. Since taxis cost almost nothing, we loaded the bicycle into a light van taxi and headed out of town to his apartment. I had a shower to wash the dust and sweat off my body. I say shower, but it was hardly a shower room, more a toilet with a shower-head hanging down in the middle. You washed yourself standing immediately next to a Japanese-style, hole-in-the-floor type loo. This was a real eye-opener. I had never been to mainland Asia before. After bathing we had dinner. We were joined by Yan, a Chinese Malaysian student, and Lee, from Korea, and headed for the university campus. In a restaurant packed with students, I got my first real taste of China. I was baptised with real Chinese food.

Food is the world – yum yum China
    Sautéed lettuce
    Sautéed pork with red peppers
    Shrimps in oyster sauce
    Garlic pickle
    Largo. A local beer *(xiao qu)*
    We ordered item after item . . . A wide range and large quantity of food was laid out before us. Very Chinese! The food tasted exquisite. The real thing was so much better. *Hao che* (delicious!). I ate more than enough! How excellent, I thought, to have such a cornucopia of delicious cooking and for it to be the norm for the Chinese.

    I was moved to remark, "I can't believe how tasty real Chinese cooking is. I was told to be careful of Chinese food before I left, but I can't see anything wrong with it at all!" To which Watatsune retorted, "Being delicious is one thing, getting diarrhoea is another."

    Spot on cue, diarrhoea since morning! It was just as

Watatsune had said. One shouldn't underestimate Chinese food. Apparently the water and oil used were bad. From here to the Mongolian border, I ate with gusto, and was to suffer intense diarrhoea. In the morning I had dumpling soup from a nearby stall. I promised to meet up with Watatsune again and then set off on the road straight to Beijing.

Perhaps I had got used to the air and the smells in China, because I felt more relaxed as I cycled than I had the previous day. I was also able to take in the scenery around me better. A row of trees on each side of the road stretched away into the distance. The road cutting a straight line ahead of me was surrounded by open farmland, a blanket of green. It looked as though they had just finished the spring planting.

Dandelion-like seed-heads were dancing along in the breeze. They found their way into my mouth and throat. This went on for ages. Was this a magnificent gesture of welcome from springtime in those immense spaces of China? (I later learned that these were poplar seeds.) The honking of horns didn't let up. Watatsune had told me that, according to Chinese traffic rules, when an accident occurred, then the party which did not use their horn tended to be at a disadvantage when it came to assigning blame. To look at it another way, as long as they sounded their horns, drivers clearly reckoned they could avoid any blame. With these thoughts in mind, I noticed a large group of people ahead, surrounding a car and a truck, which had been in a head-on collision. Horns had not been ignored in the incident and it was pointless for those involved to discuss it. They had simply been going too fast. However, I had been able to foresee the potential danger posed by the vehicle that was closing in from the rear, thanks to the sound of the horn, so

I had no grounds really for muttering what a racket the driver was making and telling him to shut up. The trucks overtaking me were filled to overflowing. This was true generally in China, but these were hugely overloaded with bricks, and sacks full of grain. The domino effect could easily topple the lot. I was both surprised and terrified at how the trucks carried their loads without dropping them. Early afternoon, feeling hungry I stopped at a roadside café. Not speaking Chinese I resorted to writing down what I wanted to say. This was the first café, and this was my first attempt at written communication.

Chinese not possible speak, can writing speak
Fried rice is there?
– Have Dumplings
Fried rice want

The old man nodded.

Mmm . . . delicious. Rice is great stuff. My tummy welcomed the arrival of food. The old man and woman, the older brother and sister and their children, all looked after me warmly with gracious, smiling faces. Any feelings of mistrust were quickly forgotten. It was hot, about thirty degrees. Exhaust fumes and the horns of passing motorcycles and other vehicles intensified the heat. Many passers-by cheered me on. Cars, motorcycles and bicycles travelled alongside me, urging me on. I realised that, all in all, China was a pretty good place. My spirits rose as I rattled along. Drinking Coca-Cola and Sprite alternately fuelled me to Beijing. As I approached Beijing, cycle tracks started to appear. These grew wider and wider and in the centre. Although they were only on one side of the road, there were even cycle tracks as wide as two car lanes. The cyclist was king here. It was heaven. It took an hour to find a hotel in the centre of Beijing, a huge city with streets lined with tall buildings. Even here I could read some Chinese characters. But my knowledge was limited and it took some time for me to find a hotel. Or perhaps Beijing was really that big. The hotel I eventually found was the Tianten Sports Hotel. The name was good enough for me. I was told that the price was 288 yuan (one yuan was about 10 cent).

"Expensive!" I wrote.

'All right, 200 yuan in *renminbi* (RMB), the "People's Currency," came the reply.

Beijing Journal – Ireland in Beijing

I braced my hung-over body and leapt into a taxi. We headed for the hotel where I was supposed to meet Conor O'Clery, Asia correspondent of the *Irish Times*. As described on the phone, a westerner wearing a blue denim shirt and jeans sat in the café in the front lobby. He was tall and heavily built. Open and welcoming, he oozed intellectuality. He had been a correspondent in Washington prior to Beijing and I was surprised to learn that his predecessor was Joe Carroll. I had been introduced to Joe by Gene, my Sporting Sinatra, whilst I was in Dublin. Joe had taken over from Conor in Washington and here I was in Beijing talking to Conor. He said that he thought he had heard of Gene, which made me wonder whether the world was a small place, or whether it was simply becoming more entangled. Prior to Washington, he had been Moscow correspondent and given that I was heading for Russia, I couldn't help but feel that things were getting more and more curious. During his time as a correspondent in Moscow, and whilst he was covering the Gorbachev visit to China, the broad avenue (Jianguomen Avenue) in front of this hotel had been flooded with demonstrating students leading up to the events in Tiananmen Square. He had dropped his voice during our conversation and when I asked why, he told me that foreign correspondents and diplomats often gathered in this hotel and that some of the bellboys were security police. We chatted like that for an hour or so, then went to his house (which he also used as his office).

Guards, wearing uniforms, stood stiffly on platforms at the gate to the compound where diplomats and foreigners lived. Further on we went through a door into a western-style mansion. It was as though we had taken just one step and found ourselves in Europe. I was introduced to his wife, Janna. She was Armenian Russian, the two having met whilst Conor was working in Moscow. Her family and relatives lived in Krasnoyarsk, one of the points on my journey, so I got addresses and telephone numbers. She promised that she would give them a ring in advance. I was really grateful. This circle of acquaintances just kept on growing. It's been said many times before, but it really is a small world. (I had no way of knowing at this time to what an amazing extent these connections would help me during my trip.)

There was a photograph on the wall of his office of Conor with Clinton in the White House. No ordinary guy then. "On the Russia-Finland border there's a shop selling Irish goods. That's something to look forward to!" This sounded positively like a fairytale. We left Janna and walked over to the embassy building behind their house. On the upper part of the front of the massive, creamy yellow building, an Irish harp had been painted in gold on a blue background. We went under the emblem into the building, where I was introduced to Frank O'Donoghue, the First Secretary. He was a shy but gentle man. "Why not have the Gerry Ryan Show call you from Ireland here at the embassy? We'll fax that you've arrived in Beijing and are here at the embassy. Come back this evening, when it'll be morning in Ireland," he suggested.

(I wasn't anyone special, let alone Irish, so I felt a bit reluctant for things to go this far.)

I returned that evening. The call came through to Mairead Carr's office. Mairead is a member of staff at the embassy.

"Hey, Yaz! How're you doing? How's China? Any accidents yet?"

It seemed like Gerry was hoping something untoward might have happened even though I'd only been pedalling for two days. "China's great. The cyclist is king here. Cycling around is so easy. It's paradise. Nothing has 'happened' as such to me, but I have got one problem. Chinese food has got to me and I've had diarrhoea since the off."

"I've got diarrhoea, too, Yaz. Solidarity!"

"We're really mates now, Gerry!" (laughing)

"The Gobi is just ahead of you now. Having climbed Mount Fuji with your bike, you'll survive."

Mairead then spoke to Gerry and things livened up. Staff on the Gerry Ryan Show passed on some great information to Mairead about the Christina Noble Children's Foundation (CNCF), which had its head office in Ireland, but was active in Ho Chi Minh City and Ulan Bator. The staff of CNCF in

Dublin had heard the programme, and had said that they were interested in supporting me in some way as I was going into Mongolia. Mairead immediately called Ulan Bator and spoke to someone called Wendy in the office there. We were given details for someone I could contact when I reached Mongolia. I had no idea what sort of organisation this was, or how they might support me, but it was good news anyway. I had something great to look forward to when I got to Ulan Bator. I was overwhelmed by the friendliness and generosity of the embassy staff, including Conor and his wife Janna, Frank O'Donoghue and Mairead. All this for someone who was a nobody, not even Irish.

Beijing sketch

Beijing is home to a wide range of nationalities and customs, a melting pot of people and culture. The entire city seems to be constantly on the move and whilst this gets you going, if you go with the flow the atmosphere at street level is unhurried and relaxed. There is no sense of danger at night, even when you walk around alone. The number of people is staggering, but add bicycles, motorcycles, cars and other vehicles and the picture is unbelievable. They clatter endlessly round Beijing, the 'big city', honking their horns, shouting abuse and leaving clouds of dust in their wake. And amidst this clamour were the taxi drivers. Their driving was all over the place, but they never took a wrong turn and they never made a fuss over the fares. What moved me most were the taxi drivers waiting in a long queue at the station. They were careful to cut their engines whilst waiting and would not start them, even when the taxi in front moved forward. They got out and pushed, keeping one hand on the steering wheel. If only taxi drivers in more advanced countries would care for the environment in the same way! I suppose they actually wanted to save fuel, but still!

I ate and drank too much. This meant frequent visits to the toilet. I got a surprise at lunch-time when I used the toilet in a department store. Four loos were arranged around a room about 12' by 15'. No dividing walls, no doors. Three men were sitting on the toilets, shitting and chatting away. Deeply embarrassed, the urge to poo instantly dissipated. This was too public a toilet!

To the Great Wall . . . an anticlimax

The going had been terrible since morning. To push my motivation further down, there was torrential rain and thunder. In the congested traffic I was sprayed with water, sprayed with mud, even sprayed with rubbish. I pedalled on in desperation, and was relieved to reach the outskirts of the city, only to lose my way in an area of slums. I was surrounded by rows of workshops. There was rubbish everywhere. It stank. Old men on bikes carried rubbish, scraps of food, oil, and indeterminate putrefying slop in tin drums. I guessed they were carrying it from the inner city restaurants of Beijing. They dumped their loads in gutters and along the edges of paddy fields. I was bogged down on a mud track. I sensed danger in the looks I was getting from people in house doorways. They looked nasty to me. Places like this, just outside cities, were the most dangerous. I must have cycled through this neighbourhood for about forty minutes before I emerged, grateful to be alive. Breathing a sigh of relief I took the 'cycle track' beside the highway heading northwest, only to look back and see a strange old man following me on a bike. He pedalled silently, keeping about ten metres behind. He gave me the heebie-jeebies. I decided to try and shake him off by stopping at a café. Inside there were several guys wearing military gear. I was in a foul mood so I ate swiftly and demanded the bill. 50 *yuan*. Too much, I thought for fried rice, soup and a Coke. When I asked to see the menu again, the proprietress appeared and said that 20 *yuan* would suffice. Japanese cyclist could read Chinese characters and would not be fooled that easily.

* * *

The road suddenly started climbing from there. Full of food, I dragged myself onto the bike and resolutely set out on the long and winding ascent. With the rain, this was good training. Later, when I was nearly on the point of giving up, the Great Wall came into sight. Sure enough it was huge and long. But the shape of the wall remained indistinct in the rain. No matter, there was a real air of mystery about it. Gazing at the wall, mulling over the long history that linked China and Mongolia as I pedalled along, my back tyre slowly deflated. I had a puncture. (The first in Eurasia!) The rain wore me out. Sheltering from the rain at a small station nearby while trying to repair the puncture, station staff and one or two others appeared and kindly helped out, chuckling at me. I was grateful. I'd had it. Nothing decent had happened that day. So I hopped into a hotel. I didn't care if accommodation cost a hundred *yuan*. Body and soul were in need of refreshment. It seemed that I was the sole customer. I found peace in a so-called 'group room'. It was a single room with seven beds on the floor.

At last I heard the wind in The Great Wall.

As I crossed The Great Wall it seemed like the events in Beijing, particularly the things that had happened at the embassy, were now far beyond the Wall and behind me. Japan lay further beyond and across the sea, keeping a distant eye on me, just.

April 23rd and the rain, which had been falling since yesterday eventually let up. In high spirits I changed into a short-sleeved top and shorts. Then a strong north-westerly wind started blowing. This was a head-on. "Shit!" I muttered, straining away and right on cue again, another puncture. Today it was the front tyre. Busy days these. Repaired the tyre in a gale. This was miserable. I hardly merited the attention, but about ten people, drivers, motorcyclists and cyclists had gathered and surrounded me. They looked at me with great delight and were laughing. All I wanted to do was to tell them to leave me alone. Just then a man of about thirty tapped me on the shoulder, shaking his hands saying that I was 'Doing it wrong. Doing it wrong!' I told him if he was so smart, he should do it. I handed him the wheel and, hey presto, he did it! This was truly a kingdom for cyclists. Any passer-by could probably run a successful bike repair business if they put their mind to it. Amazed at his speed and dexterity, I shook his hand and gave him a hug. Thanks a lot! Master! Off I went again. My spirits soared with the wind, albeit head-on. In fact it was almost gale-force. On top of that my stomach was empty, so I had to stop at a restaurant run by a lovely old man and woman. They prepared some warm water in a bucket so I could wash my face. I ordered fried rice, as usual, and they started cooking it (as they did not have any prepared). The gale outside was head-on so I was in no hurry. I thought I would relax and wait it out with my rice. The fried rice came with sautéed beef and aubergine. I overate. However much rice they cooked, though, the wind wasn't going to stop. It just got stronger and stronger. The road went on and on, up and down. The wind was so powerful it stung my eyes, even when I wore my glasses. I pushed the bike uphill. I couldn't generate speed going downhill. In fact I had to pedal. When I reached the bottom, I got off and pushed. This was repeated over and over again. Up and down, on and on, up and down, up and down, endlessly. In desperation I found myself muttering, "I must have cracked it now". I didn't care how many hills I had to climb. The next moment I arrived at Huai'an, my target that day. After forty-six kilometres of going up and down, I was left feeling very down. I'd had it for the day!

I had wanted to mull over this project, to think about myself, but so much had happened every day that I had hardly had the time. Still, there was a long way to go yet. Time yet to take it easy and think things through.

To the Mongol world

As I approached Inner Mongolia, fields gradually changed to open pasture. I saw sheep and shepherds and I felt closer to 'Mongolia'. Now and then there were great cracks in the red, red earth. Patches of grass grew here and there. The occasional road sign indicated forestry plantations and young trees ran along either side of the road. The road suddenly started to climb. On both sides I noticed walls, not unlike the Great Wall, on top of which I saw what looked like observation platforms. I was now approaching Inner Mongolia. Being only about four days' cycle ride from Beijing, Mongolia was clearly really close to the city. The Mongolians must have invaded China regularly, pouring in like rain then turning for home after looting and pillaging. Through history, rather than simply being afraid, the Chinese must have decided that they had to construct the Great Wall out of a sense of absolute terror. But this was no place to dwell on the ancient history of China. I had to struggle on up this hill. A slope like this, with a load like mine, was really hard work. The scenery, though, was magnificent. Mountains pressed in. Sheep dotted the landscape. They looked like *gomashio* (sesame seed salt) spread over the mountains. I climbed unsteadily onto the stone wall beside the road, which looked like the Great Wall in miniature. The hill I was climbing reached a summit at 1,450m, just at the border with Inner Mongolia. So I had climbed exactly 600m from the town below where I started my ride that day.

Goodbye, Heibei Province. Hello, Inner Mongolia. I drifted down the perfect hill. There was no need to hurry. I just let go. The scenery changed to a barren land of red earth. Ascending and descending endlessly, what looked like the town of Qahar was now visible to my right. I had found it basically by following people's instructions. It was a large town, packed with people. I was, as usual, the alien loitering like a street performer in downtown Osaka. A crowd would gather the moment I stopped, particularly kids. Surrounded, chased, I dived into a hotel. I wrote my details in the guest register book and asked how much it would be. Two hundred *yuan*! My face expressed incredulity. The price dropped to one hundred *yuan*. The receptionist explained that the manager agreed to discount the price because I was a foreigner. But they had known I was a foreigner from the start, so had overcharged me. It made no sense. I felt the shadowy presence of security police in every big town in China.

Then, of course, there were the pigs one came across everywhere in the villages in China. There were a particularly large number in the town of Oahar. Huge pigs shuffled around in every corner, snuffling up leftover food and rubbish. Brilliant street sweepers, they left absolutely nothing in their wake. They gobbled up anything not needed by humans, grew fat on it, and ended up in Chinese woks. Whilst this was tragic, it was thoroughly ecological. I couldn't help but respect those pigs.

Van Morrison *Be Thou My Vision*
HYMNS TO SILENCE

It might begin to seem that all I have written about is the riding and eating, but if I hadn't pedalled I wouldn't have got anywhere and if I hadn't eaten, I couldn't have pedalled. End of story, perhaps! Anyhow, when I wasn't eating I was, by and large, pedalling. This really meant that the times when I stopped and ate were very important opportunities to meet and chat.

I had a wonderful encounter at lunch-time in a restaurant. Eating simmered mutton (I was in Mongolia now!) and dumplings, I chatted with the owner and his friends and family. I told them that five *yen* coins were supposed to be lucky in Japan, and that I had offered one to Shikoku, one of the boys staying there. In return I had received one of the rosaries he held. They said that it was a happy charm in

China too. (From this day on I made sure I wore the bracelet, although I had no idea just how beneficial the bracelet's power would be.) There was a great atmosphere – we looked at each other's photos, they rode my bike and I let them sign my helmet. These were to be the first and last signatures in China.

The Irish flag was painted on the front of my helmet and the Japanese flag on the back. Between them lay the Eurasian continent, that 'Japan – me – Ireland gap'. I wondered whether, as the people I met along the way signed this area, the emptiness in my soul, too, would be filled as I travelled on?

A rest day in Jining

After faxing status reports to Bridgestone and the Gerry Ryan Show, I thought I'd go for a leisurely stroll around town. Jining is one of the bigger towns in Inner Mongolia, and the area in front of the station was packed with buses going in all directions. There must have been about sixty buses. The area buzzed with travellers, workers in transit, touts and food sellers. People, people, people. I liked this 'Chinese' atmosphere. I walked along the broad avenue from the central station to the hotel. Cars, bicycles, motorcycles and horse-drawn carts surrounded me. Fishmongers had spread fresh fish out on vinyl sheets on the ground. Were they river or lake fish? (It struck me as odd, because whichever they were, I certainly hadn't passed any bodies of water on my way so far. The countryside had been bone dry). There were people selling sunflower seeds (Chinese people seemed to love munching on seeds), vegetables, fruit, beer and woks. There was just about everything. Even petrol. Not from a pump, but from a small tanker. Brilliantly coloured flags fluttered on the roof and there were characters that said 'YY Mobile Petrol Truck'. There were pay-as-you-go mobile public toilets, too. I returned to my room and had a nap. I slept well. When I got up I tightened the screws and nuts on Rocket Boy ONE, oiled up and checked everything. Looking at the map, I noticed the road travelling north from Jining getting very narrow. This obviously meant that the asphalt disappeared. So I had to double-check that everything was in good working order on the bike, and switch to off-road tyres.

The Pogues *If I Should Fall From Grace With God*
IF I SHOULD FALL FROM GRACE WITH GOD

The same thing happened this day as happened when I left Beijing. After resting, rain started the moment I left town. The sun wasn't smiling on me and that was for sure.

A narrow road to the north lay ahead of me. This was the final stretch of asphalt road. I reached the town of Qahar Youyi Houqi after about 70 kilometres. Beyond the town, the hard road ended abruptly. I was surprised to find an old man on a motorbike who spoke Japanese. Hard to believe in this out-of-the-way rural spot in Inner Mongolia! I pedalled on, but after a short distance I saw the same man turn around and come back.

"Up ahead, where the road splits, don't go straight on. Straight ahead you'll hit some mountains. You'll have to detour around by taking the road to the right."

Tomortei on the right road

He came all the way back just to tell me this. I expressed my gratitude in Japanese, whereupon the man shouted, "For China-Japan friendship!" and with wheels slithering around in the mud, set off back the way he had come. I pedalled after him, sliding around the muddy road. I intended following his detour instructions but I couldn't. I had no choice but to follow the road up the narrow valley into the mountains. Keeping one eye on the north-westerly compass direction (I might as well have used the road itself given that there was only the one heading in that direction), I passed through many villages, but the road just seemed to go on and on with no sign of the next major town, Tomortei. It seemed that somehow I had lost my way (but how?) in the rain and the mud. At least I had the opportunity of observing life in Chinese villages. They were crumbling. The houses were crude with earthen walls. Beyond the fences were pigs, cows, horses, sheep, chickens, dogs, people with dark, grubby faces, donkeys and wells . . . I travelled on and on but still didn't reach Tomortei. Getting worried, I stopped to ask a young man the way. He pointed into the distance and indicated with a finger, while sniggering, that it was 100kms, the swine.

I'd had it for the day. I waited until it got dim under the stands of trees that lined the rice fields, then erected my tent for the first time in China. I could hear a tractor working away, even after darkness had fallen. Dogs barked endlessly. It would be a bad night.

* * *

Having cycled such a long way the previous day, surely I would arrive in Tomortei soon? I set off in high spirits, but

after pedalling for an hour I still hadn't arrived in Tomortei
or anywhere else. I asked direction from villagers, truck
drivers, and young men on motorbikes and without
exception they pointed in a south-easterly direction. From
the map I figured that I had to be heading northwest, so this
was in completely the opposite direction. I was really fed up
now. I was at my wits' end. Worse than that, I was
bamboozled. There was nothing else for it but to carry on
heading north. (For no apparent reason, this seemed like a
reasonable compromise.)

I had been travelling off-road since yesterday. After the
rain the road was heavy going. Progress was made
increasingly difficult by the fact that I had lost my way. To
top it all a strong wind was now blowing straight in my face.
The cattle ambling around the fields beside the road stared
at me as I struggled by. Pitiable I might have been, but all I
could do was laugh.

*When what you are aiming for remains obscure, every
little thing tires you out. It seems to be true of life in
general. But there are times when we must push on,
even through the darkness.*

For some reason or other I pedalled on and when at last I
arrived at Tomortei, I worked it out that I had travelled
about sixty-five kilometres since setting out. I was tired. But
how on earth had this happened? I suppose I had made a
series of mistakes after I went off-road the previous day.

After lunch, I took the road north. To my delight the wind
started to come from behind. It was actually pushing me along.
My compass showed I was heading northwest and the wind

was fair. The road was firm, with few potholes or bumps. Yes, yes, yes! All at once conditions were perfect. I flew along. Even though I was cycling with a huge load, I unexpectedly found myself in top gear. Yowzer! I was travelling across a green and gold grassy plain. Mongolian scenery had replaced the red earth countryside of the preceding days. It no longer felt like China. This was cycling at its best. It was ideal. Bicycle journeys are characterised by moments of elation and depression. This morning I had been in utter despair. Now I was as high as a kite. I crossed a railway line, noticing that I was on the right track. I could have gone on and on, but time is time and I called it a day. I had camped last night, but the prospect of camping today was far more attractive. I was in the middle of grassy plains. I wasn't stuck under some trees between rice fields. There was absolute quiet apart from the occasional train that passed on the line a short distance away. I hadn't seen a single car on the road since midday. The silence was exquisite. The journey was finally beginning to turn out as I had hoped.

The sun rose across the tracks and I woke with it. The grassy plains were absolutely still. A mist had closed in and I could almost hear water droplets forming. I saw several horses ahead in the distance. Grazing freely, they wandered below the blanket of mist. Gazing on that quiet, dreamlike scene, I breakfasted on Chinese bread and sausage. A refreshing sense of peace filled my entire being.

Wild Oscars *Moments Of Value*
FISH

I struck camp and set off. The road was dirt, as usual, but

felt good as there were few bumps. Small creatures on the road ahead were startled, and fled, as I approached. I saw a big marmot (weren't they called *tarvaga* in Mongolian?). Lizards scuttled away on all fours to avoid being run over. Hedgehog corpses lay here and there, signs surely of the wilder side of nature starting. Later I noticed what looked like a town up ahead. I asked a shepherd whether this was Sonid Youqi and he said that yes, it was just over there. Coasting along, it took ages, even though the town had seemed so close initially. In fact I covered about twenty kilometres before I arrived. This must have been an illusion of sorts, created by the dry, crystal clear air and the extraordinarily good visibility. The suburbs were, as usual, strewn with rubbish. Even puppy corpses were scattered amongst the waste. This sort of scene, typical of China, would soon be behind me. When I went into one of the unbroken line of restaurants alongside the road, the old men inside, smelling of drink, flocked out and gathered around me. I was constantly bombarded with questions, as always. The manager of the establishment pushed his way through and dragged me to one side in an effort to have them leave me alone. There was no rice ready to fry, but the old man started to cook some rice anyway. He was so generous. Whilst I ate my sautéed beef with coriander, he told me that the next town, Erenhot, which was on the border, was one hundred and twenty kilometres away. As I had already covered seventy kilometres, getting there today would be out of the question. I asked for the bill but the old man told me not to bother. A friend next to him said that he was a living Buddha and that I should put my hands together as if in prayer. So I did. I placed my hands together, demonstrating my gratitude, whereupon the old man led me out. He rotated his two arms violently in a symbolic gesture. I presumed he meant this as some sort of encouragement. The road turned to asphalt as soon as I left town. Doubtless someone somewhere had deemed it appropriate to have a posh road near a national border. Whatever the reason, I cycled along the smooth road, my speed steadily increasing. I got into the high twenties (km/h), and even into top gear. Visions of Erenhot spun in my head. Life, unfortunately, is not quite so straightforward. A strong wind suddenly got up. Blowing from due north, the headwind slowed our (Rocket Boy ONE and I) progress. Then a cold rain started falling. Was this the final ordeal I would have to endure in China? My speed and my spirits plummeted.

A tractor with several children on the load platform overtook me, and then stopped. They told me they were Mongolian Chinese. They all had bright, smiley faces. The father gestured, asking if I would like something to eat. I indicated that, in all honesty, I was stuffed. The tractor disappeared over the horizon and I immediately regretted not accepting. It would have been nice to stay with them. I had no clue as to what would happen up ahead. Rain showers continued intermittently. The wind eased off gradually, but to my consternation, the surface on both sides of the road was now entirely sandy earth. I had mulled over the appearance of the asphalt road and concluded that this had been laid down because the road was approaching the border. But this seemed not to be the case! Not even a dirt road, this was little better than a sand road. This was the Gobi. This was it. I wondered whether I could even think of erecting my tent here. Pedalling along, these concerns running through my mind, the distance to Erenhot gradually closed. I wanted to be there. The urge to get there suddenly overwhelmed me. Let's go for it, I thought. Let's go mad. If I could make it to Erenhot, then I would have cycled two hundred kilometres in a day. Remembering the dirt road I had cycled along that morning, however, this seemed a reckless undertaking. Still, I had to try. I lost all reason. This would be the last leg in China!

Ironically, the sun seemed to set unexpectedly quickly that day. Soon I was in total darkness. Threatened by cars thundering by, I was pedalling along inside the white line on the hard shoulder, when I suddenly flew from my bike, headfirst onto the sandy ground. I remounted and set off holding a Maglite to illuminate the road ahead. I crept along slowly in the darkness. The lights of on-coming vehicles were blinding. One truck coming the other way stopped and started flashing its headlights. Calling to the driver "Stop it!" I fell off my bike for a second time. The moment I fell, the truck started moving and then drove off. What the hell had the driver been up to? That had been a really nasty thing to do. At least I had fallen onto sandy ground, which was far better than going head first into piles of excrement, rubbish, or a mound of broken glass, I suppose. Gathering stuff was a big thing in China.

I eventually reached the town, but not knowing where to go, I had to follow a car. The kind driver guided me all the way to the hotel. What a great guy! When I at last got to the Erenhot municipal hotel, the clock showed ten o'clock. I was a wreck as were my mind, my body and my bike. Rather than congratulating myself on how well I'd done, I felt it would perhaps have been more sensible not to have pushed myself quite so hard. I was knackered, but food had to come before sleep. I wanted to celebrate the last leg in China with a beer. Not only was this my last day in China, but I had cycled across the country without having had any accidents. China, and the Chinese, had been pretty good really. I had all sorts of memories and thoughts about what had happened. The toast at that moment, however, was:

See you again, China!

See you again, fried rice!!

3

Heaven and Earth; Mongolia so fine

Traders from Ulan Bator carried cardboard boxes of all shapes and sizes towards the waiting train. Arms and legs carried or shoved on board everything from instant noodles and soft drinks to clothing and electrical goods. Just the sort of hustle and bustle I expected to find at a border station.

Standing on the platform with my bicycle, a Japanese voice suddenly asked,

"Going to Ulan Bator?"

I said that I wasn't – I intended crossing the border by train, getting off at Zamin Uud, and then cycling to Ulan Bator from there. This clearly surprised the petite woman who had spoken to me. Her eyes opened wide and her face turned pale with shock.

"Come on. Let's talk about this on the train."

With that she helped me load my bike.

My companion warned me that the Gobi Desert lay ahead, and that it was a real desert. There were no roads, let alone houses. Unless there was a nomad ger, there would be no water or food. It was incredibly hot during the day and freezing at night. Strong winds blew continually. What on earth was I thinking about, trying to cross such an inhospitable place by bike? It was far too dangerous.

Bayalma wanted me to stay on the train to Ulan Bator. She implored me not to cycle. She was currently studying at Ulan Bator University, but her home was in Zamin Uud. Being local, she obviously knew what she was talking about, and her warnings had been given with such an open, honest expression, that I began to feel genuinely worried. But my mind was set on cycling to Ulan Bator. (Bayalma spoke Japanese, having studied the language when she worked for a Japanese construction company in Mongolia several years previously.)

The train stopped at the border and visas were checked. Any worries I had were lifted when I saw the broad smiles on the faces of the officials who checked our passports.

Arriving at Zamin Uud station in the evening, I alighted and stood on Mongolian soil for the first time.

'Standing on foreign soil' is a cliché, but it describes perfectly the situation I found myself in. The earth I stood on was hardly soil, however. It was sand. My feet, and the tyres, were stuck in sand. A cold wind blew. The station hotel, which Bayalma had told me about, cost three thousand *toglog* (about 4 euro). The room was big enough for four people, and was reasonably clean. Bayalma, who had been so concerned about me, treated me to dinner at a nearby restaurant. We had mutton stew (I think). This was Mongolia for real now. I didn't see the price, but I felt it was quite dear. I wondered if she could manage. *Bayarlalaa* – thanks!

I decided I would head to the telephone office and try calling Ganbator, the man from Ulan Bator I had met on the ferry from Kobe. It seemed that the telephone office was the only means of making calls from the town. Outside the hotel it was pitch black, and the cold wind continued to blow. There were buildings in the town, naturally, but they were few, and those that had been built were not very high. With no barriers, the wind whistled through the town. It left my hands numb. Then there was the sand. The sand stung, forcing me to avert my eyes. Crunching sand between my teeth I turned in the direction of the telephone office. I became keenly aware of the cruel environment I was in. How on earth would I cope with what lay ahead? Bayalma sorted out the telephone and did the dialling for me. The familiar voice of Ganbator at the other end sounded far away. "Anyway, take care and make sure you get to Ulan Bator safely. That's all."

I could imagine his worried expression. Bayalma had a word with Ganbator, muttering again and again how worried she was. I don't understand Mongolian, but their concern communicated itself to me quite clearly. They were such kind people.

I talked late into the evening with Bayalma and Bator, my room-mate who was importing second-hand cars from China to Mongolia. More than anything else, these two Mongolians struck me as being entirely natural. If I had to compare them with the Chinese, I would say that the way they spoke, the way they laughed, their gentleness, and their manners, in fact everything about them was more easy-going and calmer. Being with them just felt normal. It was as natural as air. It was remarkable to find how, in just a few kilometres over a border, people could be so different.

Both of them wrote words of encouragement in Mongolian on my helmet. This would be a charm, they told me, that would help protect me against harm on the journey.

I eventually turned in, but was kept awake by the sound of the cold wind relentlessly whipping the sand along outside. When I woke up, all was peaceful outside. The wind had ceased and blue sky filled the window. Mongolian blue. Heaven suddenly seemed closer. It was seven thirty. Bayalma stood in the doorway holding a pot of Chinese cup noodles. They had come, as promised last night, to see me off and brought the noodles for my breakfast. Was this kindness typical of Mongolians, I wondered?

Bayalma and Bator looked worried as they sat and watched me slurping my noodles.

"Wouldn't it be better to go by train?" They persisted in trying to stop me cycling, but I really didn't want to go by train. I wouldn't. More importantly, I wanted them to explain the route to Ulan Bator to me. I felt that even a rough explanation would suffice. When I asked Bator, he confessed that this was exactly why he hadn't said anything, then proceeded to draw the following map.

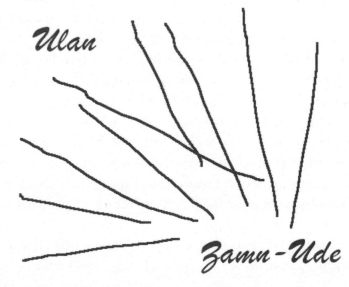

In other words, it didn't matter which rutted tracks I took. Even if I switched between them I would reach Ulan Bator eventually. His explanation was more like a puzzle. There was an important trick, however. This was to keep the Trans-Siberian railway line in view. If only I could do this, I would be all right. The two of them remained worried until the moment I left town. They returned on the train to Ulan Bator that evening. "We must meet up in Ulan Bator." With this promise I sallied forth. I started pedalling across the Gobi under a cloudless blue sky. As anticipated, the tracks were rough, but the sand was firm enough. Where had the sand come from last night? The rutted tracks I was cycling along had clearly been made by vehicle tyres and so were compacted. What would the road to Ulan Bator be like from here? How would the days work out? I felt I was facing my first real challenge.

Getting through each day was my immediate target; getting to Ulan Bator was my interim target. Achieving them would be more than enough to occupy me. I felt it sensible to quietly ignore my bigger ambition, to reach Moscow, as well as my overall aim of reaching Ireland, for the time being. The vastness of these spaces was quite overwhelming. In the mornings it seemed as though I could just sail away into the blue yonder. I felt I could touch the sky it was so close. It made no sense, but the feeling was real. I believed I could reach out and touch the sky. Below the blue sky lay the endless earth, stretching further than the eye could see. My situation made me feel like I was the filling in a 'heaven and earth' sandwich. The Gobi had started in Inner Mongolia, but I hadn't felt like this then. Something intangible had changed. Was it the air or the smell? My mind reflected on the unfathomable as I pedalled on. There must be 'something' here which humans can just not understand

I spotted a number of camels up ahead. They made a real desert scene. I decided to take a picture of them but at the crucial moment I heard a vehicle approaching from somewhere behind me. I wished they would go away, but the vehicle got closer and then started sounding its horn. The atmosphere changed completely. A dark blue Pajero stopped near me in a cloud of dust. Looking at it I noticed the smiling faces of Bayalma and Bator inside. Bayalma was holding up an oddly familiar booklet. My passport? Idiotically, I had gone and left it at the hotel reception. What was I like? *Bayarlalaa*, Bayalma, Bator! I dread to think what might have become of me if they hadn't noticed my passport and arranged a vehicle to bring it out there. Or if they hadn't found me . . .

"Now we'll have to meet up in Ulan Bator, won't we?"

Laughing, the two of them set off in the direction they had come from.

U2 *Where The Streets Have No Name*
THE JOSHUA TREE

The camels disappeared. Time to gather my strength and set off again.

Further on I spotted a white object. On closer inspection it looked like the skeleton of a cow. There were more, further on. This time the skeletal remains had skin still attached. They belonged to a horse. It seemed like the animal had sustained an injury and died there. The bones lying scattered all over the place were a reminder of what a harsh, unforgiving environment this was. In these temperatures, and with such low humidity, I would have to be extra careful too. This was no joke.

The road was not soft sand, but it was tough going. It meandered on and on over undulating hills. Climbing the hills was very hard work. The downhill sections were steep, which meant I had to keep the brakes on. The smell of rubber increased my concern about the brake pads melting. On top of this the sun was intense. My skin was scorched. The hot air was bone dry. I had three water bottles, but my throat remained parched, however much I swallowed. Gulping the water quickly depleted my reserves. Whilst I had about three litres of water in my reserve bottle, my fears of dehydration persisted. I should have been sweating in proportion to the quantity of drink I was consuming, but no sweat lay on my skin. I assumed that the sweat was evaporating as soon as it appeared. I had a runny nose, but I couldn't keep stopping to blow it. So I cleared my nostrils with a short sharp blow, only for the contents to end up spattered on my thigh and arm. Even this dried to a crust almost instantly. All I had to do was to brush away the desiccated debris! This world of ultra-low humidity had its bonuses!

As I dwelt on these and other banal thoughts, a flock of sheep came into view. They were gathered around a well, drinking. I gestured to the young shepherd scooping up the water that I was thirsty and would like some too. With a broad smile, he deftly raised the bucket and proceeded to dump the contents over my head. The water was refreshingly cool and tasted absolutely delicious!

During the afternoon I spotted a tiny hamlet beside the railway line. Without a moment's hesitation, I raced over, drawn by the prospect of water and human contact.

People immediately gathered round me. I had become sick of the crowds that surrounded me in China, but was thankful for the attention now. Apart from the shepherd I had met earlier, the only other encounter I had had since setting out today was with camels and bones. (Needless to say there had been no cars.)

One of the elderly, a more senior woman, brought me cup after cup of Mongolian tea. I was even given biscuits made with sheep's milk. They had a slight smell to them, but looked like they would give me energy. As I ate them with gusto, a young man produced some dried sheep's innards. One of the rules of the road is, as everyone knows, that you'll never understand the locals if you don't eat the local food, but I drew the line at this. Both the smell and taste were too overpowering. One mouthful and I gestured that I'd had enough. These folk were so relaxed – they didn't even talk. They just gathered round me and smiled.

Tonight was my first night under canvas in Mongolia. About to hammer in a tent peg, I was startled to see a snake. I'd been caught off guard by the light brown skin that I had taken for earth until it suddenly moved. "Demon," I muttered to myself.

By dusk a blanket of cloud filled the sky. The sun slipped through the gap between the clouds and the horizon. Gazing at the golden evening glow as I slurped broth from my emergency ration pack, a speck suddenly appeared on the horizon. The dot, which seemed to be moving in my direction, looked like the silhouette of a horse and rider. The next moment a tall young man astride a white horse stood in front of me.

Unable to communicate using the written word, we

resorted to hand gestures and body language. I showed him my helmet, trying to explain, among other things, that I was *'Yabano, Yabano'* (Japanese), but I'm not sure he understood me. He just smiled. A few moments later he disappeared. I must have been watching the horizon for half an hour or so, when the same man reappeared on his white horse. This time he had a rubber bucket in his hand. The bucket was full to the brim with water. When I had had my fill, he filled my three water bottles. He beamed at me, and then rider and white horse disappeared over the horizon.

Following instructions carried to her by Hermes, the messenger of the gods, the nymph Calypso released Odysseus. Odysseus then set sail across the high seas on a raft he had made, but the raft was destroyed in a storm called up by Poseidon, the sea-god. Odysseus was adrift on the sea for two days and two nights before, with the help of goddess Athena, he eventually reached an island.

Was there going to be rain that morning? Rain in the morning was the one thing I hated most. Why was it raining anyway? I was surrounded by sand! I am in the middle of the desert! Depressed at the thought, I stuck my head through the tent flap to discover that it wasn't rain but condensation. The sound that I thought was rain had been sand pattering against the sides of the tent. Seeing how the sand had piled up around the cooking utensils I had left out after cooking the previous night, I guessed that the sand had been blowing around all night. Sand had even got in under the flysheet.

The day broke brilliantly clear again. I felt elated. The

bumps, the twists and turns, the undulating hills – they all inspired me. I had got used to them. I felt ready for anything now. If I hadn't been pumped up like this, I would only have felt sleepy. It was full steam ahead! Then, all of a sudden, my tyres sunk in sand. What was going on? This looked like real sand. It was terribly deep today. The tracks I had been following came to a halt here and I could see nothing ahead, to the left, or to the right.

All I could see in the middle distance was an enormous sand dune. I was in a grumpy mood. I supposed I would be all right. After all, I had been following faint tracks like this up to now. The sandy track might be doing a disappearing trick, of course, but I didn't dwell on this thought.

The pedalling was really tough. It was not only the wheels I was concerned about, I was afraid that the entire bike, with me on it, would get stuck in the sand.

Given the depth of the sand and the weight of my load, all I could do was push. A minute later I was exhausted. Imagine walking through a kindergarten sandpit pushing a bike with a load weighing 50 kilos. Who on earth would begin to contemplate doing anything quite so crazy? I pushed for a minute then rested for two. Even so the effort tired me out. Then it occurred to me that there might just be a track somewhere to the left or right. I left the bike where it was and wandered around but found nothing but sand. 'Take it easy.' I thought to myself. Then I shouted this to the sand.

I decided I had no choice but to walk and push. I had to maintain a forward momentum. It was blisteringly hot. Now there was evidence of sweat lingering on my skin. The aridity simply hadn't quite got round to drying it off. I steadily consumed my water, but the draughts I took were never fully satisfying. There was a significant difference in the effort involved in walking and pushing, and pedalling. Bicycles, after all, were designed for the pedals to rotate constantly, and for the wheels to be driven by the pedals. I would have died for an ice-cold gin and tonic! For God's sake, how long was this going to go on for? Where would I end up? It was scary.

Images of sand filled my mind . . . spotless white turbans wound around the heads of Arab caravaneers crossing the deserts . . . the trailer-man, Tadashi Nagase . . . now there was a great man . . . amazing how he crossed the Sahara Desert pulling a trailer . . . mountains of sand on a construction site, shovelling sand and mixing it with cement . . . Abe Kobo's book 'Woman of the Dunes' . . . what was that insect which the hero came to search for on the beach?

How long had I been pushing for? An hour or two, more? Time was being swallowed up by the sand whispering as it disappeared. One thing was clear: I was now adrift on this sea of sand. Any hope that sooner or later the tracks would appear evaporated like a mirage. A split second later the sand stopped.

U2 *Who's gonna ride your wild horses?*
ACHTUNG BABY

To my relief the ruts had reappeared. But where on earth was I heading? I seemed to be going a bit too far to the left. The next moment the track started veering off to the right. I gave up. I didn't care which direction I was heading. I was fed up with the sand. Then I saw a stationary white object in the distance. It was a ger, a Mongolian nomad tent! An oasis! I left the tracks and pedalled ecstatically in that direction. Yee-hah!

"Usu! Usu!" ("Water, water!")

The man in the ger came out to meet this stranger bowling excitedly across the plains towards him. He opened his arms in a welcoming gesture and led me into the ger.

The ger was more spacious inside than its appearance had suggested. It wasn't huge, but it was spacious. How did the Mongolians achieve such a feeling of space inside a ger? Two pillars supported the roof in the centre. Between the pillars there was a hearth and stove and some utensils. A chimney stuck through a hole in the roof. Two iron beds were arranged around the felt walls to the left and right. There was dried mutton under the beds. To one side there was a milk churn filled with water. Between the two beds, opposite the entrance, there was a small wooden table, below which there was a box containing clothes and on top of which stood some photographs. That was all. The feeling of space was created by the simplicity of the contents of the ger, but it was also related to the fact the ger was dome-shaped. The same impression of space can be found in planetariums. Solar systems can be generated on the roofs of planetariums because the dome structure encompasses such a broad spatial dimension.

On finishing a cup of hot tea, I was offered some risotto, made with mutton and simmered with Chinese rice. I ate the risotto with raw onion, and found it surprisingly good. Perhaps it was because I was so hungry, but prepared in this way I found the mutton quite palatable. I enjoyed the food so much that I managed two platefuls. The old man who seemed to own the ger brought more tea, saying, "Eat as much as you like. Drink as much as you like." Two young boys lay sprawled beside him, resting on their elbows, watching me and smiling. Another young boy was playing a flute. A woman was breastfeeding a baby, whilst other children played around me. It was a natural, wholesome atmosphere.

I had bought a copy of 'Kyokushuzan: An Autobiography' from the National Sumo Hall in Tokyo before I left, with the intention of using it as a sort of passport to get me across Mongolia. It had the desired effect, as everyone was delighted when I produced it. It was an instantly effective tool for communication, and a great help when written communication was not possible. The wrestler, Batobayal (Japanese name Kyokushuzan), active in the world of sumo in Japan, is a hero in Mongolia. There are even supporters here who call out his Japanese name 'Kyokushuzan'. It seemed sensible to put the book in the bag on my handlebars so that I could whip it out quickly as and when required. Engaging with one of the younger boys in a bout of Japanese-style sumo outside the ger, the taller boy came up and asked if I would like to ride a horse. I could find no reason to refuse. How could I turn down an offer to ride a descendant of the Mongolian horses that swept across Eurasia in the thirteenth century? The chestnut horse had other ideas. It didn't move a hair. Perhaps he didn't fancy me. The lad smacked the horse's backside, to no avail, whereupon everyone piled out of the ger and started jeering at the beast. He was a tough chestnut, but when the long-haired lad placed a rope around his neck and tugged, the horse started moving. In fact he moved away smartly and began accelerating rapidly. The chestnut was going wild. The speed and vibration kept increasing with a momentum like the quadratic function. My body was violently shaken on the saddle. It dawned on me that this was plain reckless. Falling off at this speed, with no helmet or other form of protection, could be disastrous. From Tianjing, across the Great Wall and into Mongolia, I had taken the greatest care in the saddle to cycle safely, and although I had so far travelled without mishap, I was now in danger of falling off a horse, breaking bones and putting an untimely end to my journey. This possibility was by no means inconceivable at that moment in time. First I got stuck in the sand, now this. What was happening? What was Chestnut up to? "Stop, stop, stop, sto . . . op!" I implored him. Pulling on the reins so fiercely I was afraid I might tear the horse's mouth. However, Chestnut suddenly came to a halt. We waited for a safe pair of hands, then turned round and were led slowly back to the ger. The assembled onlookers guffawed at my antics. These were the best horsemen in the world and I was indeed a beginner. They should have realised that much at least. There was no way I was getting on a horse again. I had learned the hard way.

Time to leave. It seemed a nonsensical question at the time, but I asked the young man the way to Ulan Bator. He nimbly leapt onto his horse and went off ahead of me. Astride a horse the Mongolians are very handsome. It's a noble sight. When we reached the crossroads on the grassy plain, he turned and flew like the wind back to the ger. It had been a full-blown introduction to ger life. Completely naturally from beginning to end, I was treated with kindness and hospitality as a matter of course. Being travellers themselves, looking after another traveller was as natural as breathing air for the people who live in them. If people who live in the wilderness did not support one another, life would be unsustainable. These people have lived like this for thousands of years.

The Gobi Desert continued to the next day's objective, the town of Sainshand. It would be a big effort but I'd get there. I looked forward to a cool drink, a glass of juice perhaps, when I arrived. Mm, with ice. Now that would have been great.

A fierce wind blew from morning. Dear wind, I thought resentfully, thanks so much for continuing to blow head-on. This was the final onslaught thrown at me by the Gobi, and I wasn't making satisfactory progress. Struggling along, I noticed something glinting up ahead to my left. A horse and rider were galloping steadily in my direction. The rider was an old man with a sunburned face, wearing dark purple Mongolian garments. He had sunglasses resting on the rim of his hat – the type of sunglasses fighter pilots used to wear.

"*Sainbaino* (You all right?)." His voice was deep and dignified.

"*Sain. Sainbaino?*" I replied, prompted by his greeting.

"Aah. Sain," he replied in a sonorous voice.

This was all we said to each other. He smiled broadly, then turned and sedately galloped off somewhere. I was still battling against a strong wind several hours later when, out of the blue, another horseman came flying towards me. Compared to my shabby appearance, these guys were so elegant. This time the rider was a young man wearing a jacket. Using hand gestures, and helped by my helmet, we managed a conversation. The shaven-headed young rider warned me of danger ahead.

"The track divides about fifty kilometres north of Sainshand. You must take the road to the left. If you go right, you could come across some robbers with rifles, waiting to steal your money."

"Mongolia, so fine. Mongolia, so fine."

Mongolia was 'fine'. Surely I had no need to worry about anything like that? I naively persisted in saying so, but he simply repeated, "There are good Mongolians and there are bad Mongolians." I was intimidated by the terrifying expression in his eyes.

My speed dropped significantly. The wind chose the moments when I flagged to blow even harder. To make matters worse there was sand in the wind. This contributed to slowing my progress. At last I arrived at Sainshand. Sainshand is the capital of the Dornogobi Region and is a relatively big town. Mounds of rubbish dotted the outskirts, reminding me of the rural towns in China.

I came across a couple in a community in the suburbs. The man smelled of alcohol. After asking for some water I enquired about hotels. The man grudgingly went inside and came back with some water. He then started gesturing with his fingers, implying that he expected some money. There was something frightening about the old man so I decided it would be best to break off and leave as soon as I could. I pretended not to understand and said, "*Bayarlalaa* (Thank you).' This prompted him to deliver a hard slap across my cheek. What the heck was he doing? I was tempted to hit him back but I stopped myself. This was Mongolia. Foreign soil. If something happened it would be terrible. It was time for a sharp exit.

I found a hotel and then went out to do a bit of shopping.

There was a disagreeable atmosphere to the place. Many of the people had a mistrustful look in their eyes. It felt like I was being followed, so I hastily returned to my room. My mood had deteriorated as the events of the day unfolded – first the story about rifles, then the assault, now the atmosphere of this place. I was beginning to lose faith in people. Maybe 'urban', with all its negative connotations, is 'urban', even in Mongolia.

Anyway, the Gobi was over. What a relief!

The young rider had told me about the robbers, but I wondered if he had been telling the truth? If there were robbers, I wondered where they would be. They would also have been nomads of some sort, so they were not going to linger long in one place. Anyway, when was the story about the robbers supposed to have happened? The Mongolian oral tradition, and the legendary speed of the transmission of stories, has been well known since the time of Genghis Khan, so it was likely that his story was based on the very latest information. This thought just made my mental images more vivid and my anxiety greater. I couldn't get thoughts of the robbers out of my mind. All I could do was pedal on. There would be no end to it if I carried on worrying during this journey anyway. I decided that I would do a hundred kilometres that day and so avoid being held at rifle-point. As I had hoped, the Gobi ended, and the condition of the tracks improved considerably. I managed to generate some speed. My fear of robbers was not unrelated to my haste.

For some unknown reason, I had begun to keep my eyes fixed on a point just ahead of me whilst cycling. In Mongolia it was best to keep adjusting one's vision on the far, mid, and near distances, in a balanced way, but since the previous day

I had been watching the ground right in front of my nose, about two to three metres ahead of my front tyre. This was not good. I was getting paranoid about the road. In spite of taking so much care, I ended up getting a puncture anyway (my third!). I had to laugh. The clumps of sharp, stubble-like grass sprouting out of the ground must have caused this puncture.

I eventually decided to call it a day. I reckoned I had travelled at least one hundred kilometres, so I ought to be safe from the robbers now. Where would I sleep? Prudence dictated that I didn't put the tent up. On the other hand, I didn't really fancy the idea of slogging on to the next town, only to get slapped as I had the day before. What should I do? At that moment I spotted a white object over to my right. It was a ger! Perfect timing! This was it.

Seeing what seemed to be a sheep shed, I guessed that they were a semi-nomadic family. There were two gers. A young man squatted in front of the entrance to one of them. He had a moustache and a face that looked charred more than sunburned. The fierce sun is another of life's hardships in Mongolia. The man smiled broadly, twisting his bristling moustache, and led me inside the ger. My growing mistrust of people vanished in an instant.

I was introduced to the family in the ger. The young man with the moustache, Batsaihan, was twenty-six. It was hard to believe we were the same age. He looked so much older. It must have been the severity of the natural environment, and the look of dignity that came from having to support a household there in the wild. His wife, Sarungeldo, breastfed their newly born baby, Battsu Tsaakan. The baby was bound up in what appeared to be a belt. I was told that this was 'Sain –

fine'. Then there was their two-year-old daughter, Bahtimpkh, obviously feeling a little jealous at all the love that was being lavished on the baby, and Tsagan, the mother who had come to help her daughter after she had had the baby. The evening meal that Tsagan then prepared in silence consisted of mutton risotto, dried mutton on the bone, fried bread, and mutton broth. The smell and taste of mutton which, to be honest, had been so distasteful when I first entered Mongolia, had come to taste good. Munching dried mutton when I felt tired gave me stamina. The fatty meat slipped down a treat. It was really delicious. I presented them with a shamrock sticker as a token of my gratitude. They stuck it beside the photos. I also remembered to hand over one of the sumo wrestler cards I had bought at the National Sumo Hall.

As long as there were people like this nearby, and given that there was limited sleeping space inside the ger, I decided I would pitch my tent there. This was probably the first time in their lives they had seen a tent. Everyone's eyes opened wide with delight and they started chattering to each other excitedly. Batsaihan helped hit in the pegs with a hatchet. When it was up, Bahtimpkh and Tsagan went into the tent and started tumbling around. The next moment they were out and using the tent as a trampoline! (I urged them to be careful not to break the poles. . .)

Thus we had a Mongol tent and a western tent next to each other, looking quite the thing.

It was time to bring the sheep back home. Batsaihan leapt onto my bicycle and raced off in the direction of some sheep in the distance. I could just see the solitary figure on his make-believe horse. He'd never do the day's work on that!

Meanwhile, his regular mount stood redundant. (Where had Batsaihan learned to ride a bike, anyway?)

Shortly I heard the sound of Batsaihan's voice calling "Haw . . . ho. Haaaw . . . ho", then saw him returning, followed by a flock of sheep. A mountain bike leading a flock of sheep on the Mongolian Plateau was some spectacle.

The sheep would not wander off in the middle of the night if the lambs were put inside the shed, so the work of catching the lambs and putting them in the shed began. The flock was led into a pen that adjoined the shed, where a rope, thumped on the ground, caused them to scatter. The lambs moved slightly more slowly than the older sheep and this presented an opportunity to grab them. This was more difficult than it sounds. Unless one acted swiftly and grabbed them, the lambs got away. The work literally left me covered in sweat, dust, and dung. (My pathetic tally was two lambs.)

A beautiful evening sun sank below the horizon to a chorus of lambs bleating inside the shed. Tsagan explained that, if ash from the *argal* (dried cow and horse dung) burned in the stove was spread on the centre of the forehead, babies would sleep peacefully. Lying on my side in the tent, I anticipated a good night's sleep, whether or not I had ash on my head. With the others, and all the animals, around me, I felt absolutely safe. My open-air lodgings were far safer than any hotel.

I wanted to gaze at the starry sky, but the moonlight was dazzling. It was at least as bright as the lights in a baseball stadium.

Enya *Shepherd Moons*
SHEPHERD MOONS

Meeeeeeehhhhhhhhhhhh . . .
Meeeeeeehhhhhhhhhh . . .

Morning, woolly boys . . . Milking time . . . but I had no intention of doing anything. It was much too cold. My thermometer indicated ten degrees below freezing. Early morning air temperatures had been this low since I reached Mongolia. I lay submerged in my sleeping bag like a fat larva. Only my nose and mouth protruded through the small aperture at the top of the bag. Day temperatures, however, rose into the thirties, so there was a big temperature difference between night and day.

In the morning I munched on dried mutton. This proved a bit much for me. Even when I passed wind, it smelled of mutton. Little two-year old Bahtimpkh had the job of collecting *argal* (dry manure) from the pile that had built up near the ger. Watching her as we went together to put some of the stuff in bags, I was reminded how robust the upbringing of these steppe people was, right from the start.

A boomerang-shaped cloud drifted across the peerless blue Mongolian sky. Clouds regularly drifted across the sky, but Mongolia is an ultra-low humidity environment. I wondered where the clouds came from. Perhaps the clouds were formed by moisture from Lake Baikal, and were then blown over the Mongolian Plateau?

I suddenly caught sight of Batsaihan galloping around. He was racing along after two horses, following a great arc. He looked magnificent on his horse. Sitting there alone, looking at the sky and the earth, the sheep and the horses, it dawned on me how human beings are simply one element in nature. People say that nature is vast, or that surviving within nature with such vigour shows how mighty humans are, but in reality we exist in nature on the same level as sheep, cattle, horses, flowers, dogs, and goats. Observing how Mongolian people lived, I felt this even more keenly. This was a self-sufficient, simple life. Nothing at all was wasted. Life was natural; life was a part of nature. Mongolians who lived like this, however, could hardly be considered as being the same sort of people as the Chinese (or Japanese for that matter), who assiduously till the soil and are tied to farming the land. The Chinese, on the other hand, probably regard Mongolians as footloose and carefree. The fact is that both have their own ways of living. I, too, had to follow my own path with conviction, and press on.

Returning to the ger for lunch, I found the doctor had come to visit in a Jeep. I have perhaps given the impression that life in a ger is entirely self-sufficient, but very occasionally there are visits; deliveries of water and a medical team. The only thing the doctor seemed to do, however, was have a brief talk with the family, and then everyone, including the doctor and the nurse, stood idly around. They were so *laid back*. I became slightly better at the job of rounding-up the lambs in the evening.

Batsaihan and his elder brother-in-law returned under a beautiful evening sky, leading ten or so horses. This brother-in-law was short, but stocky. Superb at handling horses, he was thirty-six years old, and his experience showed. His brothers joined us for dinner. It was a happy family gathering. Everyone got excited when I handed over a magic marker pen for them to sign my helmet. They drew letters and patterns on the backs of their hands. His younger brother-in-law asked if I would write my name on his wooden horse-sweat-scraper. Everyone believed that this ink would last forever. White teeth in happily smiling faces glittered in the dimness of the ger.

To express my gratitude for all the kindness they had shown me, I produced my Suntory Old Whisky. By the light of a candle, I measured out a shot into the cap. Everyone was very excited. More, more, more they cried. It was probably the first time they had ever tried Japanese whisky. This would probably be the last time too. They were so pleased that I could almost see my friend, Ono, who had given me the Old Whisky as a parting gift, smiling too.

Van Morrison *Burning Ground*
THE HEALING GAME

Something wasn't right.

I could see the railway far away to my right, and the tracks were obvious, so I was clearly still on course, but the compass needle had swung around to the east slightly. It was possibly just my imagination, but the question remained 'Had I taken the wrong track?' The directions the compass needle was indicating alarmed me

With hillocks dotted here and there, it was inevitable that the track would change direction as it weaved around them, so as long as I could see the railway line, I thought I would be all right. There was no need to worry. The headwind remained strong and kept blowing throughout day. The day after a rest day – there was no rest for the wicked. I disliked punctures more than the wind. My spirits plummeted whenever they occurred. After getting a puncture, I felt the wind more keenly, and my anxieties about taking the wrong track mounted. Getting a puncture depressed me more than anything. I should have dismissed these negative thoughts.

I braced myself and pedalled on, but soon noticed that the compass was pointing almost due east. Logic said that it should be pointing northwest, but that would mean it was 135° out. In this situation, I had no choice but to stick to my strategies of following the track around the hills, and keeping the railway line in sight. The track I was on was the only one, so all I could do was have the faith of my convictions.

This went on worryingly long. Reassuring myself that I was heading in the right direction, evening began to close in. The next moment a town appeared ahead of me. A factory with chimneys was sited next to the town, or was it a power station? The people walking around the town had a shady look about them, but perhaps I was just imagining it. Motorbikes roared triumphantly through the streets. Having just come from the land of the ger, I found the sight deeply depressing.

Where was this, anyway? Laying out a map I was deeply engrossed in working out where I was, when two young men wearing Nike caps rode up on horses. They told me some bad news. This was the terminus for a narrow line that took off from the main railway line, and that Ulan Bator was in a completely different direction. I would have to go back about forty or so kilometres along the track I had been following, and return to the main line. I was amazed. So my compass had been right. What a fool I had been for following the wrong railway line. I had no recollection of having passed over the tracks, so where on earth had I deviated from the main line? I had not the least inclination to backtrack across that bumpy, burnt earth. Could I go more directly from here to Ulan Bator? There were ruts leading in all directions.

Yasuyuki Ozeki

The boys with the Nike caps cackled with laughter, telling me that this was out of the question. They insisted that the only thing to do was to go back the same way. Or even better, they said, I could lodge with the Russian-looking woman they were pointing to, and even get her to have sex. The suggestion was accompanied by lascivious gestures suggesting breasts and wiggling hips. They told me to come with them, so I tagged along. They began discussing something, from horseback, with the woman who lived in a nearby apartment.

I didn't like this at all. It was a side of Mongolian youth I was not keen on seeing. I'd had enough of this sort of town. I was exhausted but I thought if I went on a little further I could camp. They had said it would not work, but I decided to try going back. I would make some progress by not retracing my tracks exactly. I would head more in the direction I should have been travelling in. There was no way I was going to retrace my steps all the way. The tracks pressed hard up against the mountains. However tired I was, I intended to put some distance between that town and myself. I had to be at least out of sight of those guys.

I was sure I had gone far enough. I could only make out the factory chimneys dimly between the mountains. At exactly the right spot there was a small lake with horses standing at the margins, drinking. It was a peaceful scene. The journey should be like this. The question remained however. What tracks would I take tomorrow? Were the ruts ahead the ones I had cycled along to get here? Or were they the bigger ones a bit further to the south? Well, I just had to press on. Acting decisively in this sort of situation could only make me stronger.

70

Odysseus, having drifted to the land of Phaiakians, falls asleep near some washing pools by a river. Athena visits the Phaiakian princess, Nausikaa, in a dream, and urges her to go there and wash her clothing. The princess provides Odysseus with food and clothing and then leads him to the town.

When I didn't know the way, all I could do was ask somebody. But as this was right in the middle of the Mongolian Plateau, people were very few and far between. Fortunately there were gers. *"Sainbaino. Sainbaino . . ."*
The young man emerged at the door of the ger, rubbing his eyes. It seemed I had woken him up. "Ulan Bator!" In response to my question, which was short and to the point, the young man pointed to the east, then proceeded to draw this diagram on the ground.

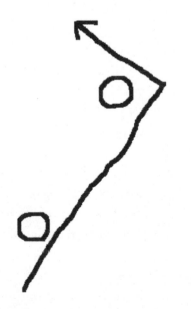

Using the map he had drawn he explained that there were two gers to the east, and that I should turn to the left after passing not the first but the second ger, and go straight ahead following the track from there. In a world with no signs or signals, gers were a great way to navigate your way around.

Cautiously applying my brakes as I made my way over wildly undulating terrain, I passed one ger, then found the second.

"Sainbainooo."

I decided to pop in and check my directions. The middle-aged man, in the middle of fiddling with a machine, adjusted his glasses, and stared at the map. My hopes grew that he might just be able to give me detailed route instructions but, as expected, this was not the case. "Go straight along the road in front here."

Onwards. I would be all right – nothing for it but to pedal on. The next moment I caught sight of three dark shadows at the top of the hill. There was something ominous about them. Oh no, I thought to myself, not that lot . . .

It was dogs. I wished they would stop their incessant barking. I had no intention of harming them. As long as they stayed where they were. What were they guarding for heaven's sake? I could see nothing. What were they up to, a three-pronged attack? They were salivating and their teeth were clenched. A dark terror enveloped me. I longed for them to go away. I was desperate not to be bitten and catch rabies out here. Would they attack me on an incline? How long would they follow me? I had been pedalling up a hill for more than a kilometre. Wouldn't they just leave me alone?

All of a sudden, the beasts ran away. I had heard about just how ferocious and tenacious the domestic dogs kept in gers were, but I had not imagined that they could be this ruthless or persistent. Anyway, I was safe. (I learned later that if you brandished anything at them, even a stick, Mongolian dogs fled.)

Something Happens *Hello, Hello, Hello, Hello, Hello (Petrol)*
STUCK TOGETHER WITH GOD'S GLUE

I continued pedalling on through the mountains. I rode over plains, over mountains, on the wind. I occasionally descended, but this section was mostly up. The highest point I reached was about one thousand six hundred metres. I was tired, but I enjoyed the changing scenery as I travelled through the gullies between the hills. Travelling through mountains brings the pleasure of seeing new vistas spreading before you as you proceed. The actors on the wide-open stage here were the grazing horses, cattle and sheep. The actors were always the same, but the stage sets, with the mountain backdrops and the lush green plains opening out between them, were a joy to behold. I was delighted to find yellow flowers in bloom. The first proper flowers I had seen since China. I noticed conical rocks piled up here and there with knife-edged stones protruding from the top. They looked like they might have been *obuu*, objects used in shamanistic rituals, so I decided it an appropriate moment to offer a prayer.

Later I passed two camels. One of them was pulling a trailer with an oil drum. The old man leading them muttered, *"Usu, usu."* and pointed his finger around a field. I understood from his gestures that he was a water-carrier. He explained that he delivered water in exchange for mutton.

I wound through the mountains all day long. When I

finally came to one that was overwhelmingly big and seemed to go on forever, I decided to call it a day.

Over to my right, ridge after ridge of mountains rolled away into the distance. Grassy plains covered with yellow flowers and dotted with grazing horses spread out below the mountains. It was a peaceful and remote country scene. I would camp here for the night.

The moment I finished putting up my tent, a rider came trotting along in my direction. He was carrying a long pole with a looped rope on the end under his arm. These are used for lassoing sheep. This rider was moving with great dignity. His poise belied his youthfulness. The young rider stopped in front of my tent, his face a glowing smile.

Mongolians resemble the Japanese more closely than the Chinese, and whilst I couldn't help treating them as 'brothers', this boy, with his fine oriental eyes and shaven head, actually looked like me when I was very young. But I couldn't remember having such a bright, shining smile. It was a lovely thought, meeting someone who looked like me when I was a child out here in the middle of the steppe.

The boy simply sat on his horse and looked down at me smiling. He remained quite still. I produced my helmet and the Kyokushuzan book and he examined them, still with the grin on his face. The big smile continued as he stood there after looking at my things. Nothing changed when I handed him a sumo wrestler card.

The only possible response was for me to smile back. This was all most pleasant, but it seemed like we could go on forever like this, so I took his photo, he took mine. Something seemed to stir inside the boy, because the next second he was gone, like the wind, over the horizon.

On the point of preparing a meal, two riders now appeared. It was the boy with his father. "How's Batobayal (Kyokushuzan) doing then?"

The old man started asking questions and then went quiet as the conversation immediately dried up. "Come to our ger and have some food. It's just over there."

He indicated a point some away across a field, but I could see nothing. I had no intention of leaving my tent there and heading off somewhere.

"Look. It's right over there. Come along to the ger."

I decided that I might as well trust them and go and have a look. Bayarlalaa. I would leave the tent there and go on my bike, with my belongings, to the ger.

"No, no. You can't sleep here. Look, there's a track over there, and vehicles occasionally pass by. Someone nasty might find the tent during the night," they said, "and turn you and the tent upside down. Stay in our ger."

Since I had gone to the trouble of erecting the tent, I really wanted to sleep there that night. All I really wanted was food. Then I would go back to the tent. He said that it was too dangerous and that I should go to the ger. I said 'Bayarlalaa', but what about the tent . . .? In the middle of the debate, the old man suddenly leapt to his feet, and swiftly pulled out all the tent pegs. Up to then I had thought I was on a flat, unbroken plain, but a little way off there was in fact a large depression, and in it was their ger. I was amazed.

The western sky began fading to pink and purple as gathering clouds chased the sun over the horizon. The sun went down, and it had started getting dark, when two herdsmen appeared following a flock of sheep. We welcomed them home. I wondered how many sheep they had.

"Four hundred sheep," the old man said proudly. From the pen they were in, eight hundred sheep's eyes looked at us in the gathering gloom, shining like emeralds.

They were kind people. Understandably finding it hard to bear the stink of my sweaty feet, they brought me some soap and water. This was precious water that had to be delivered by camel. The wife then rolled out dough made from wheat flour and made me mutton *udon* noodles. They said I should add some spices, but there was only a little left, and as it was probably quite expensive, I declined. "*Eeto, Eeto*," the kind old man urged. (I had read somewhere that they did not import spices, although techniques and cultures from far and wide had been absorbed into the Mongolian empire. It was just one of the things that had changed over the centuries.)

Their hospitality included offering me some snuff, although I don't smoke, and burning pine needles as incense. To create space for me to sleep on a bed, the young boy had to sleep on a woolen blanket on the floor. A portable radio, the family's prize possession, was then switched off. All was quiet and still. Moonlight filtered in through the window in the roof, illuminating the faces of family and friends in the photographs on the stand in the middle of the ger. A shamrock shone next to a Lamaist Buddha image.

That day the weather had been so fine and clear I felt I would be crushed under the weight of the blue sky. Sandwiched between heaven and earth, my head bouncing around as I rattled across the grassy plains, a flash of light had exploded in my head. I wondered what the single most important thing in a human being's life was? Clothing, food, shelter? Eliminating them one by one, electrical goods, cars, entertainment, etcetera, etcetera, I was left with food, family and friends. Clothing and somewhere to live were essential, of course, but when you whittled things down to the barest minimum, what was left was the need to eat food to live.

As far as family and friends were concerned, and this was rather a philosophical point, without people we wouldn't exist anyway. Wandering alone across the plains of Mongolia, being helped by the Mongolian people, I became deeply aware of this simple truth. And that was all that the lifestyle of the Mongolians really boiled down to, Food, family and friends. Spelling it out in English, all the words began with F. The 3Fs. It had a nice ring to it.

* * *

The wind began to blow from behind me for a change, pushing us along. After the first few hours, pedalling of the day, the uphill track eventually ended, to be followed by a long downhill section. My mind, body, the wheels, the sky and the earth, everything was turning in harmony. Purple flowers dotted the plain and marmots fled as we approached.

Getting through each day was my immediate objective. The next major objective was Ulan Bator and far beyond that lay Moscow, a big objective. When I got up in the morning, I focused on this, on how far I had come and the fact that if I covered the planned eighty kilometres today I would reach my next objective – Ulan Bator. My spirits soared.

Luka Bloom *The Acoustic Motorbike*
THE ACOUSTIC MOTORBIKE

I found myself climbing steep mountains again. My next

objective was very close, but getting there was proving tough and effectively dampened my enthusiasm.

The state of the track was poor. The tracks between the mountains were narrow, and sharp stones got lodged in my tyres. It was so bumpy and hilly that I had to keep the brakes on most of the time. The wheel rims were almost too hot to touch.

In spite of these difficulties, I gradually began to feel more excited. I had to treat impostors, be they ruts or stones, with equanimity. At times like this I believed I could deal with whatever nature threw at me. I could push the bike. I could walk. I could deal with punctures. I could do it, come what may!

Cookie break. From the ridge I was on I could see mountains stretching away into the distance. By no means very high, the smooth-sided mountains, topped by gently sloping ridges, felt substantial, and in the clear, dry air, appeared to close around me.

I began to go downhill and soon found myself entering a valley. The next moment I noticed the tracks multiplying. One, two, three . . . They came in from all directions. The track I was on became smoother and broader. It felt good.

To my right I could see dark brown fields, with folk energetically tilling the soil with hoes and other implements. I had seen no cultivation of any sort since leaving China. It looked rather strange. Next I saw a collection of metal masts towering into the air ahead of me. I counted, one, two, three . . . there were nine in all. They must have been all of thirty metres tall. I guessed they were television masts.

I was in no hurry. I had cycled about sixty kilometres, so I must have been close to Ulan Bator. Munching into the bread I had put aside for my lunch, I caught sight of something bright glinting in the middle distance. It was strange seeing an endless line of cars driving along at high speed (I must have seen fewer than ten cars since leaving Zamin Uud), and even more peculiar that there were no dust clouds following the cars as they sped along. Amazing!

My anticipation grew, and, with it, pedal power. Yeah, yeah!

Being reacquainted with my long lost friend made me realise what I had been missing. Long time no see, partner. I wondered how she had been. I hadn't seen her in such a long time that I didn't recognise her straight away. I looked at her, said that I had missed her, and whispered that she had grown fairer since the last time I saw her. Back together, and overwhelmed, I dismounted and kissed the tarmac in gratitude. I rolled onto the skin of civilisation and glided smoothly on my way. I wondered why the asphalt there was split into small sections.

Then a road sign in English appeared. ULAANBATAR 20KM. Onwards!

Next I came across a river. There was a bridge too . . . and trolley buses. There were likely to be foreign tourists in town. How long had it been since I'd seen tourists?

"Hi!" A voice had hailed me from across the street. It was Christine from Liverpool in England. She was a fan of bicycle touring, but was then on a backpacking trip in Mongolia. Christine and Julie, her trip mate, had just been wondering if they might encounter some touring cyclists when I had suddenly come into view! I agreed to meet up with them and the rest of the group for dinner that evening.

Ulan Bator hotel was too expensive for me, but a young man who spoke fluent Japanese at the front desk of one of the hotels kindly took me along to a cheaper establishment nearby, the Toshin Hotel. I was pleasantly surprised at finding such kindness in a city. It was a western style hotel with white walls throughout. I wondered if it would be acceptable for me to wander around the hotel in such a smelly state. Just lying on it I managed to turn the floor of my room black.

I had my first shower in eleven days. Hot water! I had never imagined a shower could feel so wonderful. I made a mental note to try and remember this feeling of gratitude. But what of the filthy water that was disappearing down the plug? Off went all the sweat, grime, sand, dust, mud, and snot I'd picked up in the Gobi Desert and the rest of Mongolia. I went with Christine, Julie and two of their Swedish friends, to an Asian restaurant in one of the hotels, the Edelweiss (this struck me as a completely inappropriate name), where I set about refreshing myself with Heineken. It was fantastic. The fresh tomato and pork dish I had was indescribably delicious.

The Swedes then retired and the three of us proceeded to the Tuborg Bar. There I indulged in the dream that had haunted me in the Gobi, a gin and tonic. This went some way to quenching the thirst that had been building up to that moment.

"Here's to no more punctures!" It was a tarmac road from here to Europe, so I anticipated having no more punctures. Agreeing wholeheartedly, Christine signed my helmet. However I wondered how long I could travel without a puncture.

The Christina Noble Children's Foundation

"Your room will be occupied by another guest today, so we kindly request that you vacate your room by eleven o'clock." The woman on reception spoke in faltering English on the telephone, but the message was brutally clear. The breakfast had been a western-style buffet. Having eaten to my heart's content, I had just finished hand-washing my filthy, sour-smelling clothes, and hung them up around the bed and in the window, when I got the surprise call. When I checked in I remember saying that I wasn't sure how long I was going to stay, but that it might be two or three days. I got the impression that they had any number of empty rooms at the time, so what on earth was the problem? I got over my frustration but was left feeling a bit stupid.

I had already telephoned the local manager of the Ireland-based Christina Noble Foundation, Wendy. I had been introduced to her on the Gerry Ryan Show when I was in Beijing. She had said that she would come along and meet me straight away, so I decided to simply leave the hotel. I'd had enough of this hotel.

In the middle of packing up, a call came through from reception saying that there was someone waiting for me. The woman waiting for me was short and had hair flecked with grey. Approaching with a broad smile, she emanated a sense of tremendous energy. This was my first and abiding impression of Wendy.

"Congratulations for making it to Ulan Bator safely."

I followed the Russian Jeep carrying my baggage to her office on my bike.

Being an Irish organisation, there were two Irish staff based there. Annette, a typically charming Irish woman, and Orna, who faintly resembled Enya, were both nurses. They told me that they were the only Irish people living in Mongolia. Wendy was English. The formal name for the foundation is the Christina Noble Children's Foundation

(CNCF), an organisation whose mission is to support children.

Annette outlined the nature of the work the foundation did, and explained what had brought me here. The role of the CNCF is firstly to provide financial and administrative support for children who do not have the money to obtain a passport and identity papers, both of which are required for admission to a hospital in Mongolia. In addition, children can come along to the clinic there and have a medical check-up free of charge. There is also a ger village on the outskirts of the city where street kids and orphans can stay. Each ger has someone who acts as a mother figure looking after the children. Children leave the gers when they reach eighteen. CNCF also helps with the rehabilitation of children who, living in poverty, have ended up getting involved in crime and have been in prison. Some kids receive special schooling there. Finally the foundation searches internationally for parents prepared to adopt, and for sponsors.

The CNCF office in Mongolia had opened in October of the previous year. The first centre in Asia had been established in Ho Chi Minh City. The foundation's headquarters is in Dublin. The staff there had found out about my trip through the Gerry Ryan Show, and had said that if I was passing through Ulan Bator and needed any help, then I should get in touch with the local office. I was very grateful indeed for this kind offer.

In addition to Wendy, Annette, and Orna, it so happened that one of the foundation's international managers, Carol, was there, as well as a host of Mongolian staff. From the moment I met them, they treated me as if I was an old friend. I was at my wits' end about where I was going to sleep that

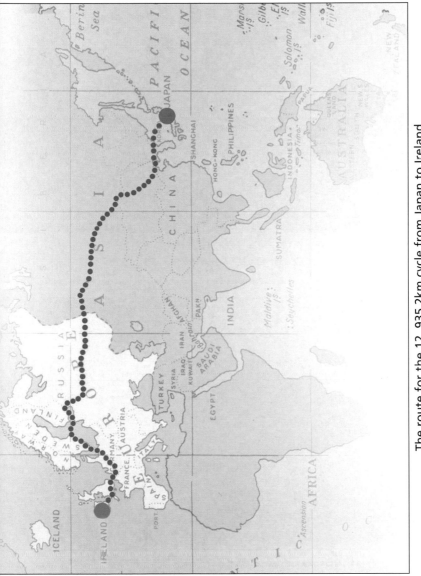

The route for the 12, 935.2km cycle from Japan to Ireland

CHINA • Helpful connections. *Irish Times* Asia correspondent
Conor O'Clery and his wife Janna

BEIJING • Evening time in Tiananmen Square

CHINA • Bright shiny faces of the friendly Mongolian Chinese

CHINA • The Gobi desert ahead – goodbye China, hello Mongolia!

MONGOLIA • Inside the Ger, a traditional Mongolian house

MONGOLIA • Eastern and western tents meet

MONGOLIA • An encounter with my childhood

MONGOLIA • Time stands still. The water man

MONGOLIA • Hardworking staff of the
Christina Noble Children's Foundation

SIBERIA • Friendly fishermen offered me food and drink

SIBERIA • Meat market in Irhutsk

SIBERIA • Landmark painted bus stop

SIBERIA • Dinner al fresco. Cooking fish at the side of the road

night, so every member of staff started thinking about a place for me to stay. Unfortunately, the prices were beyond me. This caused considerable consternation. Wendy came up with an idea. "We're all girls, and so most probably won't stop talking, but if it's all right with you, Yasu, you're welcome to stay at our apartment." I was delighted at this invitation and accepted wholeheartedly. I eventually ended up spending six nights with them, but not, I might add, to indulge myself in the company of the Irish girls I was surrounded by. Thus far I had managed to avoid getting ill, and been able to pedal strongly, but the moment I reached Ulan Bator my condition deteriorated. I got a cough. My joints ached. I felt dizzy. The Mongolian doctor at the CNCF clinic diagnosed a cold caused by over-tiredness. The body is a high-fidelity instrument and, relieved at being surrounded by such kind and gracious people, any stress I had been suppressing suddenly seemed to manifest itself. As far as getting ill was concerned it was good timing. The two nurses in the house even administered a children's cold remedy and some pills.

One afternoon, whilst recuperating, I at last heard from Ganbator. It seemed he had been worrying about me ever since I had spoken to him on the telephone from Zamin Uud. To reassure them that I was in a reasonably healthy condition, I arranged to meet up with him together with Bayalma and Bator, the friends who had pleaded with me to travel to Ulan Bator by train. The reunion party was at a Korean restaurant called Seoul. I was happy at the prospect of the reunion, and the taste of *kimchi*. I felt so elated that I forgot my wretched body and downed three beers.

That night I came out in rashes all over. The itching was unbearable. I knew I was not supposed to, but I couldn't stop myself from scratching the itches. This made the itchiness even worse. It was driving me mad, so I went next door and woke Orna.

'Could you give me something. Anything! Maybe some string I can tie my hands up with so that I can't scratch myself," I pleaded.

Orna remained half asleep, with her back turned to me. An hour or so later she appeared in my room. I was on the point of despair by then.

"What on earth is all that wriggling for? Put on some gloves, then if you rub yourself with those it won't be so bad, will it? Scratching the itches with your nails is not helping at all. It's silly." With these words, Orna returned to her room, rubbing her sleepy eyes.

It seemed that the problem had been caused by a combination of cold pills and alcohol. In fact it was more than just a problem. It could potentially have caused quite a dangerous reaction and everyone was relieved that it had stopped at discomfort. The doctor ordered me off alcohol until I was completely better. This I found depressing, seeing as it was a rest week . . . I couldn't complain though. What if I had been on my own? The luxury of having nurses on hand to rub lotions into my back was the sort of good fortune that has its limits. The CNCF staff helped me in various other ways. They gave me rides into town in their Jeep and even went to the trouble of taking me back to my apartment once or twice. Learning that one of the Mongolian members of staff, Ula, had a colleague who was working in the Russian embassy, I went along and was able to have my Russian entry visa date brought forward. This would ordinarily have cost me a considerable amount of time and money. I was also invited to a party, given by Carol in appreciation of all the hard work done by her staff, at a ger restaurant on the outskirts of the city. Listening with my eyes shut to the folk songs sung with deep emotion by the Mongolian staff, I could almost smell the grassy steppes.

The kindness everyone extended to me was incalculable, but it was thanks to the CNCF that I was afforded this rare opportunity to glimpse another side of Mongolian life.

In 1995, the population of Mongolia was about two million three hundred thousand. About 40% of the population was fourteen years old or less. About a quarter of the entire population lived in Ulan Bator, but it is small for a capital city. There is one wide road called Peace Avenue, for example, which although it is the main thoroughfare through the city is not particularly broad at all. The parliament building, hotels, department stores and other buildings line the avenue.

Otherwise, the only other streets are the narrow ones that lead off this road. The city being so small and having to accommodate such a large number of people means that the slum areas are expanding around Ulan Bator. With an under-developed industrial base, jobs are by no means certain in Mongolia. What does this mean for children, who make up two-fifths of the population? The number of orphans is increasing. The number of children living in manholes is also increasing rapidly. People have to put up with a severe climate; summers are hot, but in the winter temperatures can drop as low as minus forty degrees centigrade. Just to be able to eat, the children have to work in awful conditions. Some children apparently have to work for no wages. The government simply doesn't yet have the systems or financial resources to prevent this sort of deterioration in social conditions. Official

support from industrially advanced countries lags behind
support given to other developing nations. It may be true that,
as Annette said, "Mòngolia is isolated from, and neglected by,
the world."

Walking along with Orna and Annette, one of the manhole
children came up to us. He was clearly starving. The two of
them handed him some bread, and a card with CNCF details
on it. The address was written on the card in Mongolian so
that the children would know where to go. I had actually
seen many children, covered in sweat and dust, wandering
into the office. Seeing the relief on the faces of the children
was at once painful and wonderful.

I also visited the ger village where some of the homeless
children end up going to live with their new carers. It was a
truly hands-on project: setting up gers, providing food on a
daily basis, health and safety management and welfare
education for the 'mothers'. The results of all the hard work
put into these projects were clearly visible in the happy faces
of the children.

Looking at the children in the ger village, the nomadic
children I had met on the steppe suddenly crossed my mind.
These children were Mongolian, just as much as the children
out on the steppe.

I learned about much else besides this project, but one of
Wendy's stories moved me more deeply than anything else.
One brutally cold winter's day, a young boy, working as a
porter-cum-vendor at the station, was complaining to
someone he had not received a tip from. The angry customer
locked the boy in a freight car. Locked in for the entire night,
the boy suffered frostbite to both legs. They had to be
amputated. The boy spent the next four years begging in the

gutter before being taken into care by CNCF. Thanks to donations, the boy was later given artificial legs.

Wendy recounted with tears how the joy on the boy's face at that moment was more than ample reward for all the project work she and her staff had done since the establishment of the office in the middle of that bitterly cold winter. I was encouraged by Wendy's brave words when she said, "If you can appreciate the dangers that lie ahead, then you can go anywhere and do anything."

CNCF is funded entirely by donations. Volunteers do all the work. It made what I was doing feel insignificant and certainly gave me food for thought. This bicycle journey was, after all, only a personal dream.

A twenty-six year old Australian, called Chris, working as a volunteer journalist for a local newspaper, once told me that twenty-six is neither too late nor too early to see the world. It's just in time. Bayalma was twenty-six, as was Batsaihan, the man who had given me shelter in his ger. Orna at CNCF was twenty-six. Come to think about it, so was Lindbergh when he made his successful solo flight across the Atlantic. Then there was me and my bike. Who was this person who was intent on cycling in search of a dream, and who would that 'me' be once I got 'there'?

Contact with the outside world

I had maintained no proper contact with the outside world since leaving China. On reaching Ulan Bator, however, I at last managed to get in touch with Colm Conyngham at Bridgestone.

"We were worried about you, so it's good to know everything's going well. How was the Gobi Desert? Good luck from now on. The Guinness is waiting for you."

The Gerry Ryan Show.

"That's great that you're doing so well, but are you drinking properly? Booze that is." Gerry told the listeners to the show about CNCF. I would like to think that being introduced on the programme like this might just have helped CNCF in some small way.

Ulan Bator sketch

My time in UB (Ulan Bator) was spent almost entirely with CNCF. I only managed a little look around otherwise. In UB I just wanted to sleep all day long. My mind was muddled. Annette suggested that this might have been the effect of altitude. The city lies at an elevation of two thousand metres. Trolley buses provide public transportation in the city, but they are nearly always at a standstill. If there is a problem anywhere with the electrical lines which power the trolleys, the entire network comes to a stop. As it was so unreliable, I had to use the diesel-engine buses. Many of these were gifted to Mongolia by Japan and had Japanese flags painted on them. The most convenient form of transport, however, was the 'personal taxi'. These were basically just private mini-cabs. Any vehicle in UB would stop for you if you flagged it down, and take you anywhere you wanted. Fares were effectively metered by distance. For travellers such as myself, though, the fares usually amounted to virtually nothing. Mongolian meat and vegetables were on sale on supermarket shelves beside Chinese and Russian foods. A loaf of bread cost about 250T (25 cent) and 1kg of oranges cost 2,800T (3 euro). I got the impression that one would want for nothing, as long as you had money. There was only one department store. This was state-run, but the variety and quality of goods was poor.

I had been having problems with the screws coming loose on my glasses, but the woman working on the spectacles counter only had a very limited number of parts. She forced a screw in, but managed to damage the threads in the process.

Thanks to an introduction by Ganbator, I got some coverage on Mongolian Radio and Television public service broadcaster. I didn't actually see it, but apparently it was broadcast on Mongolian Radio and Television and NHK Mongolia. (I only learned about this later on the road.)

Out on the steppe, the moon had been so bright it had obscured the stars in the night sky, but in UB, I was fortunate enough to glimpse the stars. The night sky over UB is supposed to have the brightest stars of any capital city. The stars were packed so tightly I could almost hear them whispering to each other.

Restarting

Wendy, Orna, and Annette stood together on Peace Avenue, wishing me well at the tops of their voices. The green, white, and orange balloons attached to the baggage on the back of my bike bobbed in the breeze. They almost seemed to be waving to my three friends as they gradually got smaller and smaller.

I had stayed in Ulan Bator quite a long time. Now it was time to leave everyone. I felt sad, but it felt great to be back in the saddle again. The wind blew away the gathering cobwebs.

Ulan Bator is such a small city. Within thirty minutes I found myself pedalling into the country. When you talk about Mongolia and the country, you're really talking about having to use tracks, but from Ulan Bator onwards it was tarmac. Drifting along looking at the country rolling past, was just wonderful. Three cheers for tarmac.

Greenery started to increase too. During the six days I spent in Ulan Bator, the season had moved on perceptibly, but more than that, the landscape had changed entirely. There were mountains with trees growing on them, natural dams, flowing rivers, more vegetation. (Insects had also increased). It looked really attractive. I could hardly conceive of this as being the same Mongolia as the country with the Gobi Desert. The horses drinking from the rivers here even looked happier.

With my rest days over, and even though I should really have been convalescing, I was spurred on by an increasing sense of determination, my speed increased, and the distances rolled by. I ended up cycling one hundred and forty kilometres that day.

I reached a roadside café at just the right time for dinner. I was interested to see that they had places like this in Mongolia too. Or was this a sign that I was getting closer to Russia? After dinner, I asked the owner if I could put my tent up behind his house. They all helped me put it up. *Bayarlalaa!*

On the point of hitting the sack, I was called into the house. They were waiting to toast me with vodka. Cheers! Straight. I was surely getting closer to Russia now.

There were even road signs here. I was quite surprised to find them in this part of Mongolia. As I was studying one with interest, a young man approached me. He asked me to come with him. He beckoned me in the direction of a café. It was crammed full of people. Everyone spontaneously started shouting, "Hey, *Hapon* (Japanese guy), Ireland." I was amazed. They went on to say, "Mongolia, TV, NHK . . .", gesturing that something had been broadcast earlier. It seems that I had appeared on TV the previous day. When I thought about it, I recalled how there had seemed to be something different about the people I had pedalled passed, the drivers and pedestrians. Perhaps that was just my imagination, but I had definitely been on the TV.

They kindly lavished Russian-style soup, meat dumplings, and apple juice on me. These were truly precious moments.

I started out again full of hope and joy. Just as the hills started, four boys came running up. With their satchels I guessed they were on their way home from school. Without my asking, they started pushing my bike. They pushed it several hundred metres, all the way to the top of what was quite a steep hill. It was so refreshing to see their smiling faces as they pushed the bicycle along with undiluted glee. Their joy was infectious. Pressing on, I found myself having to deal with a powerful wind. It had been blowing straight at me for a whole day, leaving me feeling frustrated and resentful. On the paved road my rolling resistance was too great. I began to feel anxious about what lay ahead.

It looked like a brilliant day. Paved road! Most of the way, it was down, down, down. I was descending at speed from the plateau. A tail-wind was blowing me along as though it wanted to jettison me from the Mongolian Plateau. Was the wind my send-off . . . my applause for having cycled all the way across Mongolia? It was top! *Bayarlalaa*! "Farewell, dear plateau, until we meet again!"

In this frame of mind the landscape dissolved. Focusing on the road, I just put my head down and went for it. It was the same after lunch. Before I knew it I was entering Suchbaatar, a town of dancing sand, on the border.

I decided to stay at the station hotel that night. In the reception I bumped into a kind old man who I learned was the engine driver on the train that ran between there and Suchbaatar-Nausiki on the Russian side. He carried my bike up to the fifth-floor room in silence. I was concerned for him, as it must have weighed a ton with all my baggage fitted to it. He then proceeded to guide me around the town – to the currency exchange office, the market and to the ice cream shop. Licking his ice cream, the old chap then wandered off. Where he went I will never know.

It was time to toast my trans-Mongolian cycle ride with well-chilled Korean and German beer in the restaurant above the station. I ate some meat, vegetables and a double portion of rice. When I finished that, I asked for more rice. I still felt hungry and I was quite prepared to pay for more rice, but they brought me another full meal instead. This was all free. Another case of Mongolian hospitality? From start to finish, I had found Mongolians to be like that, from the old man in the station to the staff in this restaurant.

I was reaching the end of my time in Mongolia and the realisation made me sad. Still, one day I would return. The thought that my tyres were sure to carry me down the road ahead to all sorts of encounters and meetings with bright, smiling faces immediately cheered me up.

Mongolia, *sain*.

Bayartai and *bayarlalaa*.

The sound of train whistles continued throughout the night.

Faintly illuminated by platform lamps, the border station was tinted green, the colour of the steppe.

4

At long last, Russia

Russians, actually smiling . . .

Was it the negative impression that had been embedded in my mind for as long as I can remember, or perhaps my lack of knowledge, or any direct experience, of Russia? For whatever reason, I felt very tense going into the country. Even though I had a formal letter of introduction, and the correct visa, I was keenly aware that I was a lone traveller, and was carrying a mountain of baggage with me on the bike. I had to be mentally prepared for whatever might befall me at the hands of dodgy characters. This included bribery.

Being ready for any eventuality, including having to hand over cash, I confess to being mildly disappointed at the radiant, smiling faces of the immigration officials, and the encouragement they gave me. Surprise was followed by a sense of relief.

Emerging from the station, my feet and tyres were at last on a Russian road. It was asphalt, thank goodness! I looked forward to a long and happy relationship with the stuff. Travelling through the mountains on the border train, I had seen more and more green vegetation, but cycling along through the trees I was aware of what a real blessing the trees were. I could sense an increase in the oxygen in the air. It was relaxing on the eyes too. I felt my body easing smoothly into pedalling. Being invigorated like that reminded me of the essential part plants play in life.

The road signs had changed completely. They were much better than signs in Mongolia. Distances were specified to one decimal point, and the steepness of slopes was shown as percentages. I was clearly in a very large country.

Cycling on over steep hills eventually brought me to the outskirts of Kyakhta. To my right I could see a big military base. Row upon row of tanks lined up in the compound. I could sense the tension of a border region.

The town started where the military base ended. The construction of the houses was not dissimilar to the houses I had seen in Mongolia. Low, timber-framed dwellings huddled together on gentle slopes between the hills. It was quite a large town. There seemed to be more Mongolian Buryats than Slavic Russians walking around. This was no surprise, seeing as I was in the Buryat Republic. Strangely, however, it was coming across numbers of white Caucasians for the first time in a long time that evoked a real sense of travel in me.

After changing some money, finding somewhere to stay and completing tourist registration forms, all of which took a lot of time and effort, I went out to see the market. Whichever country I was in I always headed straight for the market. I went there first because markets are by far the best places to learn about local lifestyles.

I saw far more goods on sale here than in Mongolia. Not only was there a wider variety, but prices were cheaper too. I bought some fruit, vegetables, buckwheat, tins of fish and some bread while ogling the sales girl (I was surprised at how attractive most of the women were). Without the language, though, I was having considerable difficulty. Not being able to communicate in Mongolia caused little difficulty, but as soon as I entered Russia it presented more of a problem. One simple explanation was that Mongolians said little, whereas Russians spoke a lot. The lady at the bank, the old lady at the registration office, the woman who ran the hotel – all of them loved talking. Since they kept talking to me, however, I was forced to respond or utter something. A sure sign I had crossed the border. Anyway, I felt I would enjoy my trip through Russia more if I could learn a word a day.

Sliding off the plateau

I was still descending from high ground. I thought I would have left the Mongolian Plateau by the time I reached the border, but the road continued to descend through forests. Going downhill I should have been happy, but the falling snow dampened my enthusiasm. I put my Gore-Tex jacket and trousers on, and a pair of gloves, but I was still cold. The cold snap really took me by surprise. For three days after leaving Ulan Bator it had been warm enough to feel like summer, and the calendar said it was the end of May. Siberia was living up to its image.

The thing that most surprised me at the start of the Russian leg of my journey was the speed of the cars. They rocketed along roads with poor visibility, narrow roads, and even dangerous sections of road where there were road works, without a second thought. Chinese vehicles had barrelled along too, the only difference being that they leant on their horns the whole time. The noisy horns were so annoying cycling across China that I found myself constantly cursing drivers under my breath. In retrospect, though, I had to concede that the honking horns helped to prevent accidents. Russian drivers were different. They didn't sound their horns. They crept up on you, silently, then roared past at fearsome speeds. Occasionally they overtook so close to me that they almost touched the tips of my handlebars. It was desperately dangerous. A collision would have meant instant death, so I had to cycle with the greatest caution.

It suddenly dawned on me that the days were now inordinately long. This was doubtless due to the fact that I was travelling further and further north. The days seemed much longer than they had seemed in Mongolia. A river meandered peacefully across the plains stretching as far as the eye could see on both sides of the road. I assumed this was the Selenga River. It was a perfect location to camp, but I was reluctant to stop as it looked so exposed. I thought it sensible to avoid making my presence so obvious. This was only my second day in Russia, so I had to remain alert and allow a little more time to get used to the new situation. I would stay in lodgings somewhere for the night.

Albina and Tora

Yesterday, looking out of the window of the café where I sat eating *pelmeni* (small meat dumplings rather like Japanese *gyoza*), I saw heavy snow falling in the moments when it cleared slightly. On my approach to Ulan Ude, the capital of the Buryat Republic in the Russian Federation, snow and hail in a strong wind almost forced me to abandon my attempt to get into the city. The force of the blast made me wince with pain. The Siberian sun was clearly out of sorts this day as well. Dull rain had been falling since morning. Feeling gloomy, I flagged going up the long, steep hills. I eventually dismounted and pushed some of the way. The rain continued past midday. I decided to take shelter from the rain at a café about ten kilometres down the road from the end of the steep hills. In the café there was a young motorcyclist, soaked to the skin, sheltering from the rain, and an old woman talking to a person who clearly worked there. The old woman greeted me with a prolonged handshake.

"*Harasho, Harasho, Harasho* (Fine, fine, fine)."

A little confused I thought she meant I was fine but as she pointed insistently at the owner of the café, I decided it had to be this large woman who was 'harasho'.

Having eaten *bozu* (another kind of meat dumpling), and some stew, I was hanging around, waiting for the rain to let up, when the 'harasho' lady came over.

"Had enough to eat? Warmed up? Come inside and have a meal with the rest of us."

I joined Albina (Madame Harasho, 45), Alexei (her son, 24), and Marina (a Buryat employee), and ate fresh Lake Baikal fish with potatoes. The fish was plain. It had not been prepared in any way, even pickled, so it tasted a little bit too fishy for me. I nibbled on some spring onions to try and get rid of the taste. Funnily enough, the onions made the fresh fish more palatable.

Being with the little group, my spirits and senses warmed, and the wet world beyond the window panes seemed increasingly unreal. There was no point in pushing on today. The rain looked set to continue. Anyway, what was the point of overdoing it? I didn't want to reach the shores of Lake Baikal feeling wretched. I had so looked forward to getting to Baikal that I wanted to be in good shape when I arrived.

"Is there anywhere around here I could stay?" I asked, gesturing in no particular direction.

"Come and stay at my house," said Albina with a broad smile.

So yet again I found myself helped by the kindness of strangers. The house I was taken to by Alexei was in a terrace that stood alongside the Selenga River. The road was on an embankment that formed a flood defence against the river, with the houses at a slightly lower level. Their house had a huge vegetable garden, in which a wide variety of vegetables were growing. There was a shed for animals at the back, housing chickens, turkeys and a pig. The livestock could provide enough food to live on in a financial crisis, and having them was a means of survival in Siberia.

Alexei said over and over, "We've no money, we've no money", but the timber house itself was solid, and there was even an outhouse. This was where I stayed. There was also a barn and a sauna room. The Russian-style sauna was heated by steam from water poured onto a baked stone. Water, heated separately at the same time, was used to wash the body. In effect, it was a Russian version of the o-*furo* Japanese bath. The sauna warmed me up. (They told me that this form of house construction was more or less standard in this part of the world.)

Tora, the husband, reminded me of the actor Ken Takakura. Unemployed, Tora had previously worked in the forestry industry and had exported timber to Japan. Along with his fifteen-year-old daughter, Naja who stood 180cm tall, the family was being looked after by Albina and her café work.

Alexei brought in a little bit of money through his night-time job as café watchman.

Returning from her job at the café, Albina busied herself with preparing the evening meal, her hair glistening. She was a powerful woman. Dinner was a plateful of the Lake Baikal fish, topped with a generous pile of spring onions, chicken pilaff, potato salad, tomato salad, and bread and naturally vodka, Russian vodka, *Russkaya*.

The five of us around the table said a toast, '*Na zdorove*', and drank the vodka straight. Down in one. After a mouthful or two, there was another '*Na zdorove*'. A few short breaths and down it went in one again. The fiery liquid delivered a karate chop to the throat, prompting a sharp exhalation of breath. Eating raw vegetables helped ease the shock to the vodka-cleansed stomach. Seeing how they drank vodka left me wondering whether they were actually enjoying the drink, or simply drinking the stuff and stoically enduring the pain.

The rate of drinking increased as dinner progressed. The impression from my first invitation to a local home, and a taste of Russian hospitality, was the simple, open, candid, gentle, yet hardy nature of the people – so *harasho, harasho*!

The party finished at two o'clock in the morning, after we had polished off two bottles of vodka. 'Shaken up' later in the night by a violent stomach ache, I instinctively rushed to the outhouse. It would be accurate to say that the horrendous bout of diarrhoea I suffered didn't just upset my tummy. My stomach simply collapsed in agony with air and water in torrents. My insides were rocked by waves of diarrhoea every thirty minutes or so. At these intervals I ended up outside, squatting over the cesspit in the little wooden shed. It was an intolerable night brightened only by the stars that shone down on me as I headed back up the path.

The battle with diarrhoea continued in the morning, with bouts hitting every thirty minutes. Pedalling was out of the question. It was no time to dwell on the prospect of getting to Lake Baikal. I spent the whole day on the toilet. Unproductive though these bouts were, I had no choice in the matter but to take action. My main dilemma was paper. The only paper they had was newspaper. Painful, sore, but still, needs must . . .

This diarrhoea was the worst I had ever experienced.

What had caused it? Had the fresh fish been off? Or had my share – about three-quarters of a bottle – of vodka done it? They were all potentially harmful, but I had followed the others. It would be foolish of me to underestimate the resilience of the locals' stomachs again. It was a horrendous baptism by vodka but my suffering was probably intensified by tiredness and by my resistance being low.

Odysseus, escorted by the princess and Athena disguised as a handmaiden arrives at Alcinous's splendid mansion. The king promises to help him get home the following day, and Odysseus sleeps at the palace.

Along Lake Baikal

The condition of my bowels improved slightly, allowing me to continue with my journey, but I felt washed out. The air temperature was chilly and in my weakened state I shivered. I cycled along with ear covers to help maintain body warmth, but the diarrhoea had left me dehydrated and this only contributed to my malaise.

I made very slow progress towards Lake Baikal. As I travelled at a leisurely pace along a level road, Lake Baikal eventually came into sight ahead. Baikal gleamed like polished gun-metal under an uncertain, cloudy sky. I took a right off the main road, down a gentle slope through silver birch trees. Over a railway line, around a harbour, I found myself walking along a sandy beach. Baikal at last . . . I felt elated, but wondered if this was only an inlet off the main lake. The beach was narrow and because the inlet was so long I really didn't get any sense of the depth and size of the lake. On top of that, snow was in the air, so I gave up, erected my tent and crawled into it.

A strong wind was blowing across the lake, building up big waves. It sounded more like the sea than a lake. In the middle of the night I was cursed with the same old affliction, and had to crawl out and squat in the icy wind. Gazing at the night sky I saw the stars looking down on me, bigger and more numerous than the stars I had seen in the night sky over Ulan Bator. They were almost audible in the unearthly silence.

The freeze-dried Japanese rice gruel I cooked using water from Baikal that evening sorted out my problem. I am sure that this was in no small measure thanks to the purity of the lake water. The excellent rice porridge helped lead to a complete recovery.

Van Morrison *Perfect Fit*
DAYS LIKE THIS

The moment I returned to the main road, the sky cleared to a bright blue. Baikal stretched away to my right, absorbing the sun's rays and glittering deep blue.

Numerous rivers flowed into Baikal from the ranges of mountains away to my left. The road went up, then down as it crossed bridge after bridge over rivers that flowed along the valleys out of the mountains. The monotony of proceeding over a succession of mountains, valleys, rivers and bridges was alleviated by views of an amazingly blue Lake Baikal. After about fifty kilometres, I came across an area covered in dandelions near a river. Time for my lunch break! Lunch amounted to biscuits. There wasn't a single café to be found. Gazing at the crystal clear river as I munched into the biscuits, I saw a red car weaving along the road towards me. It stopped nearby and four men got slowly out. There was a tubby man with a black leather jacket, a younger man with a black shirt, a man with a garish shell-suit jacket, and a young guy who remained silent. They looked menacing. I concluded that they were specimens of the fabled Russian mafia. They came towards me in a huddle, grinning.

"Fancy some lunch with us?"

Shortly, boiled eggs, cheese, special smoked Baikal fish (omul), steamed potatoes, tomatoes, cucumbers and coriander were laid out on the glowing carpet of dandelions beside the river. These delicacies were eaten wrapped up in thin pancakes. It proved to be a sensational al fresco café. The men, who had seemed rather frightening at first, turned out to be very kind. Whether or not they were mafia, they really enjoyed themselves. When we had had our fill, vodka appeared and they insisted on my drinking with them. In the event, however, I persuaded them that with the long cycle ride ahead of me I had better avoid drinking.

"Call this number when you get to Irkutsk. You can stay at our place."

Crossing the railway tracks I found myself on the Baikal shoreline. I stood right on the very edge of Baikal. How different it felt to the inlet of the previous day.

Dinner that night was *omul* fish I bought from an old lady beside the road, buckwheat boiled in water from Lake Baikal and sweet, clear Baikal water. It was the height of luxury. Clouds starting to pile up in the western sky were tied to Baikal by golden shafts of sunlight. The sunset was out of this world. Snow started falling so I crawled into my tent.

The crashing of waves on the shore hinted at the immense size and depth of Baikal, a lake so vast I could almost sense its immensity through the tent. Overwhelming was perhaps the most appropriate adjective to describe Baikal.

Baikal special

Running north to south, Baikal is a crescent moon shape, inclining slightly to the east at the top. It is 635 kilometres long, 80 kilometres wide and 1,637 metres deep. It is the deepest lake on earth, containing 20% of the planet's fresh water. The volume of the lake is more than 23,000 cubic kilometres. It is said that in order to empty the lake, water would have to flow out via the only river to drain the lake, the Angara River, for four hundred years. The river that flowed in front of Tora's house (where I had suffered with diarrhoea), the Selenga, supplies half the water that flows into Baikal. In winter the surface of the lake freezes to a depth of about a metre. Enough, it is said, for a car to drive across it. It might sound like a myth but the story goes that at the time of the Russo-Japanese war, the Russian army placed railway tracks over Baikal in order to reach the front more quickly and efficiently, sending a total of 65 locomotives and 2,000 wagons over the lake. Fishing flourishes on the lake, but two thirds of the fish caught are *omul*. They are sold everywhere. After gazing on Lake Baikal for a day, my thoughts were distilled into the idea that the lake embodied some infinitely deep existence.

Baikal was more like a sea than a lake. The mountain ranges on the opposite shore were only faintly visible in the distant haze. In spite of the mountains, I was convinced that Baikal was a sea. This was almost certainly due to its immense depth. I didn't feel threatened by the sheer depth, or feel that I might be swallowed up by the lake. On the contrary, the unfathomable depths of the lake seemed to merge with the limitless sky above, making me feel I was in their deep embrace as I sat there, looking. I was simply alone, suspended in a space between the sky and the depths of Baikal. Russians apparently dream of travelling to Lake Baikal their whole lives. Sitting there I began to understand why they feel like this. At dusk, a flock of seagulls flew over me from right to left. Three old fishermen mounted a detachable motor on a small boat and set out for the heart of Baikal.

All the natural elements are drawn down into the dark depths of Lake Baikal, where they are cleansed and then returned to the surface. My wish is that I too may be drawn down into her depths and my body, my soul and the clutter in my head purified.

The Pogues *How come*
POGUE MAHONE

I cycled along a road lined with trees covered in vibrantly green spring leaves.

The rivers feeding Baikal carry melt water from snow capping the towering mountains in the distance. Every corner of the scene before me was filled with the joy of spring. I reached the town of Baikalsk and decided it was time for a *morozhenoe* break. (*Morozhenoe* is the Russian word for ice cream. Dead cheap, dead tasty, my *morozhenoe* break was a highlight of the day.) Licking my *morozhenoe* outside the grocer's, the lady who ran the shop came out and handed me a bottle of water.

"Water. Baikal water, a present."

She held my hands tightly in hers offering encouragement.

Next a plump old boy gave me a bottle of beer bearing the label, Admiral Kolchak. His way of encouraging me perhaps? *Spasiva* (Thanks)!

If all went according to schedule I would be in Irkutsk the following day. I had been given an introduction to Sõ Kobayashi, who lived there, before I left Japan. I wanted to contact him by phone before meeting, but finding a telephone was no simple matter. I was, after all, well off-the-beaten track. Resolving to find one, I asked two ladies nearby if they could help me, and was duly escorted away to find one, apparently to somewhere 'Up, up'. We entered a building, where I was told to leave my bicycle. We then went upstairs and into the office of one of the women.

The lady said that this was the Baikalsk 'Administration', and sure enough it did look like a municipal office. She kindly dialled the number for me immediately. Sõ, it appeared, could not be found, even though the person at the other end spent ages calling round. She ended up speaking to a fellow student who was teaching Japanese at Irkutsk University. She asked him to tell Sõ that I would go along to his accommodation, and kindly re-confirmed his address. When she'd finished the call, Nadenska presented me with a set of postcards of Baikal. Clearly concerned about my well-being, she asked again whether I was eating properly.

I was moved to the point of tears to be on the receiving end of such kindness from the locals. Without a moment's hesitation, I doffed my helmet and had her sign it.

As my mood brightened, so did the scenery. The hills, however, suddenly became very tough. Struggling along I spied a couple of cycle tourists ahead. Delighted to see them I cycled up and discovered that they were a mother and a son from Holland on a bicycle tour from Irkutsk to Baikalsk. I was so happy; they were the first travellers I had encountered since Ulan Bator. They and their Russian guide informed me that the road from the town of Sludyanka, on the western end of Lake Baikal, to Irkutsk was extremely difficult going.

The mountains on the opposite shoreline gradually started to creep closer, the claws on the tip of Lake Baikal. Passing quickly through Sludyanka, with its tangle of goods trains and factories, I bought a *morozhenoe* from a shop in an area that seemed deserted. I decided to ask directions to the beach from a boy sitting on a bike nearby, looking at me and laughing. He turned out to be really kind. All I wanted was directions but he ended up accompanying me the whole way. He showed me an area that turned out to be quiet, one where I could relax. In the middle of my meal, however, a group of four other kids on bikes appeared and started to bombard me with questions. I could hardly get a word in edgeways. They were most excited by my bike. Innocent kids enjoying themselves, their faces were lit with radiant smiles.

Lively though they were, I eventually got tired of them and wished they would go home. It was still light, even though it was almost 11 o'clock. I wished they would understand, as I had to get up early the following day. I produced the sumo cards and gave them one each, took a group photo, and then, to my relief, they all went home.

The pass to Irkutsk

It was worth getting up early the following morning. After pedalling some distance up a steep hill at the start of the day's cycling, I stopped and looked back. Lake Baikal shone gold in the morning sunrise. The lake lay as still and bright as a polished mirror.

"So long Baikal. See you again some time."

My murmurs echoed crystal clear in the hushed stillness enveloping me.

It was as the Dutch family had warned. The hill went on and on. This would be challenging even without a load, but Rocket Boy ONE was loaded with about 50 kilos of baggage. It was an awful struggle, but I tried not to get off and push. Attempting to get such a heavy load up a steep hill like this was simply outrageous. Bicycles were designed to roll forward.

I climbed the Mino Mountains every weekend on my bike. On the building site, I pulled sand and concrete around on a car, and was censured by the boss for doing so. One day that summer I cycled the steep hills on the Goto Islands and nearly got sunstroke.

The continuous steep hill came to an end after about 10

kilometres. I'd done it without stopping. It was terribly steep, and had seemed impossible, but I felt it had been worth doing. Unless there were times like this then the adventure would be meaningless. I chose this life of winding roads after all, with its ups and downs.

After about fifty kilometres, I became aware of the mouth-watering smell of roasting meat. A man was grilling meat on skewers over a fire made of birch logs inside a metal box on legs. Salivating over the fragrant smells, I asked the old man if I could have one skewer.

In *shashlik* shops like that one, meat is grilled on skewers and eaten with onions and other vegetables. The filling fare gave me an instant energy boost. (There are *shashlik* shops everywhere in Russia and the shops I patronised from there on proved to be a big help in sustaining me.)

Two *shashlik* and a juice came to 50 roubles (1 rouble = about 16 cent). This was expensive. Given the location, though, I had little choice. It was roughly the equivalent of buying a bowl of *udon* noodles at the top of Mount Rokko at home. Voicing my thoughts about the price, he threw in a 7Up.

The temperature had risen to about 30 degrees. This was a huge difference to the weather at snowy Lake Baikal. By the time I reached Irkutsk, I was covered in sweat.

There were more cars, more people, and then giant factories appeared. This was the biggest city in Siberia. With such high volumes of traffic, I could imagine that accidents were the norm given the standard of driving. As I cycled along extra cautiously, the broad Angara River suddenly appeared ahead of me. I was surprised to realise that I had already come so far. Travelling over the bridge, jostling with a host of cars, I heard a woman's voice shouting from somewhere behind me. The voice got closer and closer, until the vehicle carrying the woman drew up alongside me. I couldn't understand what she was saying but I suppose, like all the others before her, she was asking where I was going.

"Irkutsk! Irkutsk!!" I shouted.

What on earth was I saying, given that I was already in Irkutsk!

She kept asking me the same question.

"Irkutsk! Irkutsk!!"

They were becoming a pain in the arse. Scrutinising the vehicle more closely, however, I noticed that a television camera was peeping out at me from the back seat. They were clearly some sort of news team. (In fact it turned out they were on their way back from covering something else and just happened to spot me.)

Anyway, I ended up being interviewed by the local TV station. As usual, I explained what I was doing and showed them my helmet.

A lady wearing sunglasses with short, blonde hair, called Elena, asked "Why?" When I replied, "For a pint of Guinness!", another member of staff brought me a bottle of the local dark beer, shouting at me, "Irkutsk Guinness!", which I duly drank. The entire story from our meeting on the bridge to the 'Irkutsk Guinness' appeared on the news that night.

Irkutsk jottings

Shredded *nori* seaweed was lightly scattered over the *kishimen* noodles.

Having existed on fried rice, dried mutton on the bone, and *omuri,* to get here and find *kishimen*, a Nagoya speciality, in Irkutsk, was beyond my wildest dreams. Tomoe Miwa, a student from Toyama University to whom Sõ had introduced me, generously shared the contents of a package she had just received from her mum in Nagoya with us. The ultra-smooth texture of the noodles was indescribably delicious.

A long time ago, during the Edo Period in Japan from 17th to 19th century, some of the Japanese people who drifted ashore in Russia wielded the birch rod in Japanese language schools in Irkutsk. One of the more famous Japanese, Kodayu Daikokuya, spent about a year in the city. Irkutsk has played a very significant role in Russo-Japanese history, and I would like to give a word of thanks to all the Japanese working there who helped me.

Sõ Kobayashi, on a short-term teaching contract at Irkutsk University, was particularly kind in looking after me and letting me stay at his flat.

Before leaving Japan, I had put together a package and arranged for my mum to send it poste-restante to the post office in Irkutsk. I had confirmed by telephone from Mongolia that the package had been sent so I set out for the post office with Sõ to collect it. The Irkutsk Central Post Office turned out to be much smaller than I expected from its formal name. In fact it was probably about the same size as my local station post office. This made me feel anxious about the safety of my parcel. I showed a brusque woman at the counter a copy of the proof of dispatch form I had with me. She handed me letters from my friends, saying that it was all she had. I knew this couldn't be right. Sõ insisted, in Russian, that she check again carefully. Fifteen minutes later she appeared with the parcel. I asked Sõ what on earth they were up to, only to be told 'This is Russia'. The following day I went along to the same post office with another Japanese friend Ken, from Oita Prefecture, to send a parcel containing some off-road tyres which I no longer needed. This time it was far more difficult. I had to divide up the parcel into three and fill in three separate sets of forms detailing the contents. They kicked up a fuss, saying that I could send some things, couldn't send others . . . It took the best part of an hour and a half. Ken told me that 'This country is about patience'. How on earth, I wondered, would I have coped without him?

Yoko Yamashita, who lived in the flat with Sõ, acted as a mother figure for the young Japanese living in Irkutsk. After leaving her job as a high school English teacher in Japan, she set off to live in Irkutsk, another of her ambitions. She was then teaching Japanese at Irkutsk University. Whilst I was staying with them, students came one after another to have Japanese lessons at the flat. Yamashita's enthusiasm did not stop at education. Being devoted to looking after young Japanese in Irkutsk meant a constant stream of young Japanese visitors would turn up, day and night. I was treated to many delicious Japanese meals. One I remember well was dried smelt. Sõ jested, saying "Russians don't eat this sort of fish, so it's sold as cat food in the market."

"Many Japanese here just go about complaining that there's nothing in Russia. The truth is that these guys lack resourcefulness. I tell them they should only complain once they've looked at the alternatives" Mrs Yamashita retorted. Then she began to prepare the smelt. Rinsing the smelt, she placed them on newspaper for a little while, then hung them up with pegs on a line to dry like socks. They were absolutely delicious. I ate them every day. Yamashita, unstintingly kind, wrote the following fine words on my helmet:

'The same sky unites us all.'

(I suddenly recalled some important information passed on to me by Sõ. Apparently pure alcohol, mixed with a tiny bit of water, was sold in Russia as vodka. You had to be careful and check what was on the back of the label. If the vodka was genuine, the manufacturing number and similar information was stamped on the backs of the labels. The dangerous stuff had nothing on the back of the label. He warned me: "If you don't check that before you get drunk, the consequences could be fatal.")

Irkutsk sketch

Any description of Irkutsk has to be made with reference to Lake Baikal which lies right alongside it. Apparently there are no water or electricity charges (hydro-electric power) in the city thanks to this abundance of water. Sõ told me this as he chilled beer under a running cold tap.

The beautiful stone architecture dated from the last century or earlier. Then there were the concrete monstrosities, unmistakable monuments to the Soviet period. As well as the larger buildings, there were clusters of ageing, but delightful Russian-style wooden houses. I wandered around Irkutsk, the 'Paris of Siberia', using trams on which you could travel anywhere for only two roubles.

Bustling crowds filled the giant central market and broad avenue in front of it, buying and selling all manner of vegetables, fruit, newspapers, books and flowers. In the crowd I spotted an old man radiating a creepy aura. Sitting on a folding chair and wearing tattered clothes he had a set of weighing scales at his feet. I asked Sõ what the old man was doing. "Oh there are many like him in Russia. We call them the

'Scales Men'. They make a business of charging people one rouble to stand on the scales and measure their weight."

"One rouble? Amazing value."

"Sure, but no-one weighs themselves."

Before I set out on my journey, Teppei and others had warned me to be on the look out for the mafia and the prostitutes tied to them. There were mafia-like figures everywhere in Irkutsk. Whilst walking along the banks of the Angara River which, with its dirty water, could hardly be called attractive, Sõ pointed out that any group of guys wearing dapper, dark suits were definitely mafia. But there were so many of them they were almost too obvious. Guys driving four-wheel-drive vehicles, such as the Mitsubishi Pajero, were certainly mafia. But thinking about it, any number of Pajeros had roared past me as I cycled along the road.

One of their lines of business was collecting money from traders for market pitches. The Russian mafia would target a shop or stall and ask the trader 'Do you need a roof?' If the answer was 'Yes, we need one', a payment would be made to the mafia, if the answer was 'No, we don't need one', the premises would be torched.

Then there was prostitution. Prostitutes are stationed in the lobby of this and other hotels. Receptionists are linked to the mafia, and guests' room phone numbers are freely available to the mafia. (The going rate is about 160 euro a night.)

Sõ pointed to a particular hotel over to our right.

Their most lucrative business, however, was buying and selling second-hand cars. Second-hand motors not sold in Japan are shipped to Vladivostok. The city is full of

Russians, Japanese, Koreans and Chinese mafia involved in one way or another in the used vehicle business. There are rumours suggesting that the Japanese *yakuza* gangs operate in Irkutsk too. Thanks to these people, Japanese cars are everywhere in Siberia, particularly in the east of the region.

An interesting aspect of the second-hand market in commercial vehicles and trucks is that, to save money on paint, owners leave corporate logos and other marks on their vehicles. This means it is easy to identify to whom they belonged earlier in their lives in Japan. I found this quite amusing.

Whilst I was in Irkustsk, Gerry Ryan was in New York.

"It's 17 degrees here in New York. What's it like there?"

"It got up to 30 degrees here today which is a bit weird – Siberia should be much colder than New York."

I also got a phone call from Colm at Bridgestone, whom I had faxed in advance.

"I can tell you now, seeing as the trip is going so well that our president and another senior member of staff have a bet on for a hundred bucks over whether you will get to Dublin safely."

Hot-blooded Victor

My joints ached, my eyes were heavy, and my head was stuffy. My nose was blocked due to the allergy medication I was on, but the other symptoms left me in no doubt that I was going down with a cold. Since there was no way I would rest up here and sleep it off, I decided to cycle on, sticking to my principle of pedalling my way back to health.

Leaving Irkutsk the road continued level for the following day and a half. My average speed rose dramatically, so that I was maintaining 19.0 km/h. That was fine, but the monotony was getting to me. Talk about endless vistas, it would be hard to equal those never-ending birch forests. The birch trees were clearly happy that spring had arrived, and looked gorgeous, but I could hardly stay awake; the scenery was so monotonous.

From about midday the previous day, the ground beneath my wheels gradually began to undulate. The undulations became very pronounced and my mood changed as the ground rose and fell. I would creep up hills then drop slightly. After repeating this pattern about five times a long, sweeping downhill section would follow. This went on and on. There were sections of gravel road. I thought the road surface would end imminently, but although I tried to make light of it, the gravel seemed to go on interminably. I had struggled along similar tracks on the Mongolian Plateau, of course, and should really have been toughened by the experience, but these gravel roads left me knackered. The gravel got stuck in my tyres and since the frictional resistance was great, I failed to make the sort of progress I hoped I would. To make it worse, vehicles bombing along the road with utter disregard for the road surface sent up long, thick plumes of dust and exhaust fumes. The temperature soared to a high of 34 degrees. These difficult conditions eventually ended after 20 kilometres, leaving me covered and choking on dust. These roads were, in reality, either under construction or their construction was at the planning stage. Imagining that the long-distance, trans-Siberian highway is a line of asphalt is somewhat naïve. It would be wiser to think of it as a challenging road that frequently deteriorates into a gravel track.

At a level crossing I was hailed by an intense-looking

man, covered from head to toe in tattoos. He sported a skinhead and a full set of false teeth (possibly gold). Seeing him spurred me on and I soon found myself at the start of a long downhill section. Below me and to the left I could see what looked like the settlement of Tulun. The setting sun, shining in my direction, seemed to be sinking serenely into the heart of the town.

A blue Lada (the most popular car in Russia by far) drew alongside me. A man with Robert De Niro facial features shouted to me across the passenger seat, and whilst I was pleased at the greeting, I had absolutely no idea what he was saying. The three women peering at me from the passenger and rear seats had broad grins. The Lada stopped. I stopped and then De Niro got out.

"Come. Our place. Sleep."

"*Daa*" ('Yes')

De Niro's real name was Victor. Although he was small in stature, he was a broad-chested labourer working in the construction industry. Later I watched Victor in the steamy sauna, slapping away sweat with a switch made of laurel leaves. My body and my exceptionally chubby legs were then cleansed using the laurel switch Victor was brandishing. Victor told me that this was a genuine Russian sauna.

Walking along the road in front of his house together after our bath, we were greeted by his neighbours. A little further on, Victor grasped my hand, suddenly looking openly angry about something. His grip on my hand tightened. When I asked him what was going on, it seems that the people we had just past had been whispering furtively about him 'walking around the place with a Japanese person'. Victor considered it unforgivable for people to behave like that. If they had something to say they should have said it to our faces, but to mutter indiscretions the moment we passed by was unacceptable. Snorting with frustration, Victor seemed to be on the point of flying off the handle. He eventually settled down, but seeing Victor getting so passionate over this issue pleased me.

His wife, Galya, cooked dinner and we were joined by their fifteen-year old daughter, Anna, and nine-year old son, Pasha. There were numerous 'Na zdorove' toasts. Vodka, vodka, vodka. Galya looked flushed. Victor looked increasingly passionate and sentimental. I just felt giddy.

Later, we all went outside into the garden to look at the night sky. The distant stars glittered as brightly as the eyes of the hot-blooded Victor.

Maighread Ni Dhomhnail *A Mhaithrin Dhileas*
GAN DHA PHINGIN SPRE

To Krasnoyarsk on 80 roubles

My stash of roubles was diminishing so I had to change some money. It was Friday, so I hurried along and got to Taishet soon after three in the afternoon. I headed straight for the bank, which I was relieved to find was still open. I went inside and asked a woman if I could change some money, only to be told, "We stopped exchanging money at three o'clock. So I'm afraid the answer is 'Net' (Impossible). Even if you need to change money for a hotel, the answer is 'Net'. If you want to change money you'll have to wait until Monday."

Clearly I would have to find another way. Had I been too persistent? The old lady turned in a huff and went back into her office. Lena, the attractive sixteen-year old who spoke English on the reception at the hotel, persuaded the stubborn old lady on the desk to allow me to pay for my stay at the hotel in dollars. Dinner that night was two tins of fish and two litres of fizzy juice. Eating two cups of buckwheat I had with me, it was all well and good lightheartedly celebrating a safe conclusion to 'Farewell to Irkutsk, Part 1', but what was I planning on doing to keep body and soul together from tomorrow? I had only 80 roubles in cash. Russian prices might be low, but travelling for three days on 1,600 yen (12 euro)? I doubted I would make it to Krasnoyarsk.

Day one

Cycling across a pass, I came to a café. A gigantic man, the owner it seemed, promptly led me back outside. He had two bears locked up in a cage, and kept them there as an 'attraction'. The bears hungrily gobbled candy given to them by their keeper. As if asking for more, the bears' paws extended and grasped my arm. Thanks to them my fleece stank of bear shit and urine. But they seemed content with the sweets that the man was only too happy to give them.

"Where did you get the bears from?" I asked.

He pointed to somewhere behind the café. He seemed to be enraptured with his bears, but it was no joke as far as I was concerned. The fact that there were bears wandering around this neighbourhood meant that I could be killed while camping. This attraction held no fascination for me whatsoever.

On the subject of wild animals, I had come across a dead wolf on the road earlier.

I really didn't need this sort of scare. Subsequently, I decided to be extremely careful about where I camped otherwise I would have been unable to sleep. I made sure that any leftover food was disposed of a long way away from where I slept. I also made sure there were no big rocks left lying around the tent, as I imagined these, too, might be used as weapons by other vicious two-legged animals. Namely people.

The proprietress of the café treated me to barley, meat broth, bread and tea all free of charge. With only 80 roubles on me I was delighted with their generosity.

U2 *ZOO station*

ACHTUNG BABY

In dire financial straits, for dinner I managed on tinned meat. As juice was out of my budget, I drew some water from a well. I tried to buy some fuel for my stove, but the pumps were shut. I was deeply grateful to be given some fuel by a man in a car parked beside the road, directly from his fuel tank.

A little further on I came across a light green one-ton truck bearing an Asahi Beer logo, parked near the road. The driver was Yura, on his way back to the town of Kansk, sixty kilometres further on.

A man in his early thirties, he couldn't stop smiling. He had on a garish sports top.

"There's a campsite on the outskirts of Kansk. You'd best stay there tonight."

I had already cycled one hundred and ten kilometres that day. Another sixty kilometres? That would be pushing it.

A short distance further down the road off to the left, I saw a parasol outside a *shashlik* shop with smoke rising from it. Great, I thought to myself, when I suddenly noticed the Asahi Beer truck parked nearby. Yura was beckoning me over from behind the parasol. He bought *shashlik* for me. I hadn't had *shashlik* for ages. It tasted wonderful.

"You'll find the *GAI* (traffic police) just outside the town of Kansk. Call me from there. I'll come and lead you to the campsite I was telling you about."

He had been so kind to me that I decided I had to cycle there, however far it was, fuelled by *shashlik*! Pumped up, I got on my bike, headed for Kansk and made it to the traffic police.

Yura turned up straight away. Wondering what on earth the campsite would be like, I cycled down a very steep hill behind the Asahi Beer truck, ending up at a large sports centre situated on flat, open ground on the floor of the valley. Yura was having a discussion with someone who looked like the manager of the sports hall. The next moment I found myself in a room in an annex to the sports hall, which I imagine was paid for by Yura. After a hot shower I found a meal had been prepared for me by one of the ladies on the staff.

White rice, sausages, cheese, ham, bread, tea, grape juice and to finish ten or so *pelmeni* were laid out. I washed this delicious meal down with many '*Na zdorove s*', in the company of Vladimir, a pipeline engineer working on a nearby site and the others staying in the dormitory. I ate more than my fill. *Harasho! Spasiva!*

Everything was paid for. I thought I would have to settle up, but they wouldn't even begin to think of asking me to pay. In a similarly generous gesture, and to my surprise, Vladimir presented me with ten rouble notes in the hope that the money would help me make it to Krasnoyarsk.

I felt like I was in heaven.

This sort of thing can and does happen.

Day two

I hadn't really expected it. Or, rather, I had imagined that it couldn't happen, but as agreed the previous evening, Yura came to the sports centre to greet me first thing in the morning. He said he would lead me, in the 'Asahi', via a shortcut to the road I had to take out of town.

As I was led through the streets of Kansk, hazard lights flashed all the way. We travelled for the best part of seven kilometres, turning right and left any number of times, before reaching the edge of town. Yura had been extraordinarily generous, right up to the very end. He was an extreme example, perhaps, but I found Russians profoundly kind. When they were angry they got really angry, when they laughed they laughed heartily, and when they drank, boy did they drink! Above all, however, was their abundant generosity.

Nollaig Casey *Causeway*
SULT — SPIRIT OF THE MUSIC

I spent the next thirty or so kilometres cycling through continuous rain. Feeling chilled, and with an empty stomach, I decided to look for a café. Coming across a bus shelter full of people, I asked where I might find a café, to be told 'Here! Here'. Sure enough, it was a café.

Families in five cars on their way home from a trip were spreading their picnics out on the ground and car bonnets.

They all became most excited when I entered (wondering,

no doubt, what in heaven's name a Japanese guy, soaked to the skin, was doing cycling through the area) and proceeded to heap food on my plate. There were robust women (who showered me with kisses), older ladies with benign smiles, several delightful girls and a number of young guys who stood silently among the energetic women. Feeling right at home with all the smiling faces, I ate the delicious food on offer – three chicken wings, a whole cucumber, homegrown tomatoes, three small onions, a hamburger (homemade), and vodka, of course. There was also plenty of bread and juice, and three pancakes for dessert. They insisted on stuffing me with so much food that I became quite concerned over the capacity of my stomach. Thanks to this fine lunch I was raring to go. I covered a good distance, about seventy kilometres non-stop, in spite of the rain.

"Enough is enough," I thought at last, and turned off the road in the direction of Uyar. I was naïve enough to believe that I would reach the town sooner rather than later, but it took ages. Normally, the best point about the location of a campsite was for it to be neither too close to the town, nor too far away. Or, to put it another way, not to be in the town, but also not to be far from it. I couldn't find such a location here. The rain was getting heavier and the gravel road had turned into a muddy track. I cycled down a steep hill into Uyar looming dimly out of the rain.

Waiting at a level crossing, a Mercedes estate drew alongside and the driver hailed me.

"Are there any hotels around here?" I asked the young man.

"I'll take you to one. Put your bike in the back," the young man replied.

When we got to the hotel, Juna (the driver), and Andrei (a

friend), kindly negotiated the price of the accommodation on my behalf. 57 roubles was reduced to 50, but they would not accept dollars (of course). I said that I would go to the bank when it opened the following day and change some money so that I could pay but the answer was an unequivocal *'Niet'*. At a loss as to what to do Andrei said, "Come to my place, have something to eat, have a wash and sleep with us."

The handsome Andrei was a young local policeman. It seems that his wife was away doing a test of some sort in Krasnoyarsk, so he had to look after me by himself. There was no hot tap water, so he added some cold water to water he had heated up, and prepared a shower using a full bucket. I scrubbed myself clean from head to toe with Timotei. Meanwhile, Andrei popped out to buy some *piroshki* and *moloko* (milk). Probably because his wife was away, it seems Andrei was planning to meet up with friends for a drink that evening.

"Sleep tight." Andrei said as he left.

Before I set out on the journey, I had imagined that as it was such a long trip, there would be times when I would get fed up with it all, but that hadn't happened once so far. Was it really so perfect?

Day three

I had planned to get up at six thirty. I was awoken by Andrei, at the agreed time. His manner was punctilious, as you might expect of a policeman. We had breakfast together then Andrei quickly got changed. He looked most dignified in his uniform. The soaking shoes I had kicked off in the hallway the previous evening had been put out on the verandah with newspaper stuffed inside them to dry.

"It's a hundred and five kilometres to Krasnoyarsk."

It was reassuring to have the distance specified so precisely by a policeman.

The sky was overcast, but it did not look as though it would rain.

Thanks to the encouragement I had received from everyone, as well as the food, financial support and accommodation, my stomach, my heart and my purse were in a comfortable way. I felt relief at not having to worry about anything. I could cycle in a leisurely way for the next one hundred and five kilometres, resting whenever I wanted to and eating whatever I liked.

The city of Krasnoyarsk lay before me as I cycled down a long, gentle hill. The sun peeped out and shone on me at long last, and the dandelions danced in profusion on the verges.

In Beijing, thinking of the day I would arrive here, the long, unknown distances I was to cycle across China, the Gobi, and Baikal, were indistinct, a hazy notion at best. But there, sitting on a bed in a pretty little room, the journey seemed like a dream. I felt a sense of relief, along with a desire to pat myself on the back. I'd made it, well done, Yasu. I'd earned a little rest.

I had a standing invitation to visit Janna's (Conor O'Cleary's wife) parents. Conor was Asia correspondent for the *Irish Times* and had been of great help to me in Beijing. Several volumes of his books were lined up on the shelves. Glancing at them, I noticed works covering the Gorbachev and Clinton eras. It was clear what a talented journalist

Conor was. Lying there at his in-laws, reading his take on events in Russia and America and Northern Ireland, a profoundly strange mood overcame me.

Van Morrison *Days Like This*
DAYS LIKE THIS

I would like to say a few words by way of introduction to my 'Krasnoyarsk parents', who looked after me for two days. The husband, Stanislav, an Armenian Russian, had worked in the Krasnoyarsk State Theatre as a shoemaker since 1940, when he was thirteen years old. He was an active veteran who had been on the job for some fifty-eight years. He now grumbled about his failing hearing but my Russian was far from proficient so we really enjoyed using hand gestures. We had a 'Stanislav and Yasu Krasnoyarsk Discourse' instead of a 'Hashimoto and Yeltsin Krasnoyarsk Discourse', an event which took place years ago.

Stanislav's wife, Marietta, also an Armenian Russian, looked after me as though she was my own mother. She prepared a shower for me and made a host of delicious Armenian Russian dishes (the meat, rice and onion rolled in cabbage was particularly tasty). On top of that, Marietta went out of her way to answer even my most insignificant questions and dealt with my problems and requests with a bright shining smile. "I'm for you," said Valera, the fifteen-year-old boy who greeted me at the entrance to one of the apartments in Stanislav's residence. This was Stanitra's grandson. At the time Conor was special Washington correspondent and Valera had studied English and had become more or less fluent. With Valera acting as interpreter,

126

his dad Volodya drove me to the post-office, the telephone exchange, the bank (where we had to wait ages to change money) and a sports shop (there were hardly any bike shops in Russia, so anything to do with bikes was handled by sports shops). I managed to do everything I needed to do, thanks to their generosity, in a very short space of time.

My main impression of the city of Krasnoyarsk, with the great Yenisey River flowing through its centre, was how dark and how big it was. Whilst the bad weather certainly added to the gloominess, the grey concrete buildings and streets were dull and colourless. Stanislav, through Valera, told me that up until 1992 Krasnoyarsk had been regarded as a city 'closed' to the rest of Russia. Prior to that time, the city had apparently been home to a large-scale arms industry.

For a few days prior to this, my rear wheel had become increasingly misaligned. I would normally have tried to balance the wheel by adjusting the spokes, but I wasn't at all sure that this would do the trick. If there was a cycle shop in Novosibirsk, I decided it would be more sensible to have the bike properly repaired on a stand.

Talking of repairs, the night I had set up camp at the end of the second day after Irkutsk, I had accidentally dropped a mosquito incense burner onto my Thermarest (sleeping mat), making a big hole in it. I decided I would try to repair the hole using my repair kit, but in the end made a botch of it. There is nothing more painful than a cushion with no air, and my mat certainly didn't encourage sleep. (I was forced to use this 'airless' Thermarest until I got new adhesive in Stockholm.)

That morning before I left, Marietta, Valera and I sat together quietly in a room with our eyes shut. They told me that this was a Russian tradition. We were praying no harm would befall me on my journey.

The wastes of Siberia lie ahead

Travelling the straight road stretching ahead of my wheels
Meandering on and on
Through silver birch forests of the taiga
They are so beautiful
Simply that
Ladas, my travelling companions,
Storm by like the wind
One breaks down
An old man fixes it with a hammer
At a café
Mixing it up with giant mosquitoes
I dine on pelmeni, shashlik, chai, borscht, piroshki, crepe, morozhenoe
At a bus stop, a Mars bar
Through the rain, against the wind, under clear skies and cloudy skies
Priama, priama, patom priama *(Straight on, straight on, and keep going straight)*
A small Aeroflot aircraft flies low overhead
Day after day my head in the clouds
In essence
The turning pedals and the wind is all there is

Until I got used to Russia or until I reached Krasnoyarsk anyway, everything was fresh and new and I didn't find it in the slightest tedious. Immediately beyond Krasnoyarsk, however, the monotonous expanses of Siberia overwhelmed me.

I could hardly stop myself from falling asleep as the road was so straight, flat and long. I wondered what the best way would be to cross the terrain ahead.

Incidents that spiced up these days included my being stopped by the 'GAI', the traffic police, out of town.

"You haven't got a gun or any drugs have you?"

Given that I was alone, and I can't have seemed anything more than genuine, what on earth were they going on about? There were so many mosquitoes, too. And they were big. The worst time was when I was putting up my tent. Before I went off the road to find a campsite for the night (in Russia you can pitch a tent anywhere), I slipped on Gore-Tex top layers over my short sleeves and shorts, pulled on some gloves, and wore a mosquito net over my head, to make sure I was completely protected from the mosquitoes. I also used an insect repellent spray around my neck area. It must have been bitterly disappointing for those hungry little critters . . .

Once the tent was up I zipped it up tight, then lit mosquito burners and got plumes of smoke going. Any stubborn mosquitoes still left alive uttered their death wishes as I squidged them one by one with my finger. (Siberian mosquitoes are big, but don't give you too bad a bite, and they tend to move rather sluggishly.) Even when I went to the loo I sprayed everywhere . . . liberally. There was no way the little fellas were sinking their teeth into my behind.

In spite of all these hassles, camping was great. The stillness of the nights, the moonlight, the invigorating sense of solitude, the feeling of liberation in the open air added to the brilliance. Touching the grass, hearing the birds. The birdsong and the wind would echo through the forests of silver birch. They sounded just like a wooden xylophone. Mornings were brilliant. The morning sun would flood the tent, turning the flysheet bright orange. Tumbling outside, I would watch golden sunrises. When the early mist cleared, grasses sparkled in the morning light. They were exhilarating starts to the day.

The Pogues *Tuesday Morning*
WAITING FOR HERB

> *Let's progress using our minds, not our feet because we are grown-ups.*

Morning, and, as soon I moved off, a man wearing sunglasses came roaring up the hill in a Toyota Carina and called out, "Where are you from?" The same old questions . . .

"Stop! Let's chat for a couple of minutes."

"No way, I've got to get on," I replied.

"But I saw you in Ulan Ude!," said the man with the sunglasses. He was laughing with delight. This was certainly amazing. "I was in a Toyota Hiace at the time!"

As evening fell I at last came to a decent-sized café. Going into the kitchen and pointing out some potatoes to a young man, he went and fetched more from somewhere at the back. "Have them," he said. He then got five onions from the storehouse next door, and some carrots. "Have these too."

We had a group photo with a young Tajik man doing seasonal work and the rest of the family. I loved the simple ethnic jacket the wife quickly put on for the picture.

The Saw Doctors *All The One*

SAME OUL' TOWN

I have been thinking deeply about my future, about an occupation, about how I can live and I am no closer to a definite conclusion, but there is infinite time to think, and there are great distances to cover. I have time and space to think things through in a calm way.

After asking around Kemerovo, a much larger town than I had expected, I eventually found the hotel. The hotel tariff indicated

Russians	31 roubles
Old Soviet Union guests	45 roubles
Others	77 roubles

Hilarious charging systems like this were common. I simply took them as they came.

Cooking in my hotel room (in a sense I had been camping in a hotel room in Russia, but it is not really on), I produced a sumptuous meal of potatoes sautéed with onions and salami, a tin of salmon, *saké*, buckwheat, chocolate cake and yoghurt.

From now, even if it meant borrowing money, I was not going to stint when it came to buying food. I just couldn't get by without some decent grub.

The banquet begins at Alcinous's mansion. Odysseus listens with tears in his eyes to the minstrel Demodocus who sings of the Trojan wars. When Demodocus then

sings the tales of the Wooden Horse, Odysseus again weeps passionately, whereupon King Alcinous asks him who he is.

The Kemerovo incident

[12 minutes past midnight, Taiga station waiting room]

A huge problem trapped me.

Having eaten breakfast and applied the Coppertone, I was on the point of leaving when I had a quick look at my back-wheel alignment. It was pretty bad. Looking at it more closely, I saw that at one point there was a split in the rim where the spokes were connected. In fact they were on the point of coming adrift. In one place the split was quite big. In another it was still small. There were also cracks in three places.

I decided that there was no way I could go on like this.

I went straight down to reception and asked the lady and a young labourer there if they knew of any shops that could help with my bike. They said that they would all be shut that day, so I decided to go and see anyway as I was not prepared to wait.

I was relieved to find the first place open, but all they had was three beaten-up old Russian bikes. So I returned to the hotel, removed the wheel and took it on a bus to a sports shop. No luck there either. There were no mountain bikes, let alone wheels. Next I got on a tram and went to a shop called Motor and Sport. It was shut. Back to the hotel and then along to a shop a young lad on a bike near the hotel had directed me to. They had no bikes at all. The young man in the shop accompanied me to a department store, but all they had were more cheap bikes. Next I went by bus to a shop in an annex to a sports hall that a member of staff in the department store had told me about but they had no mountain bikes. They said there was one shop that had mountain bikes, but if they were to order a wheel it would take about two weeks.

So I decided I would have to get a train back to Krasnoyarsk.

The tougher option of cycling on to Novosibirsk, two hundred and seventy kilometres ahead, had crossed my mind, but I felt that, if I were to attempt this, something awful might happen on the way. Although Novosibirsk was a large city, there was no guarantee I would find a wheel there, and taking a train there would not only take me right out of my way, it would also go against my policy on the trip. Far better, I decided to go back to Krasnoyarsk, which I knew had a shop with mountain bikes. I could not remember whether the shop had wheels, but in the event of their not having any, I would have to consider going all the way back to Irkutsk. I knew that in Irkutsk they even had Mavic wheels.

In my case 'more haste, more going back' might be more appropriate than the better known expression 'more haste, less speed'. It was just like the Japanese game of *sugoroku* (similar to *parcheesi*, where you can keep getting bumped back to the beginning). Two steps forward, one step back. I had little choice but to deal with a difficult situation, and accept that these things would happen. There was a train that day so I decided I would have to go immediately. I considered leaving the bike in the hotel and just taking the wheel with me to Krasnoyarsk, but on second thoughts realised that anything could happen whilst I was separated from him. I couldn't leave my trusty steed there, so I hurriedly got my stuff together and loaded up. The misalignment was so bad that the tyre was actually touching the frame. This made it too dangerous to ride so I had little choice but to push it to the station.

Anyway, when had this happened? I seemed to remember the bulging starting to get a bit worse just the other day. The spokes had started coming slightly loose in Krasnoyarsk, so I assumed that severe metal fatigue had been caused by cycling along the rutted tracks in Mongolia and the gravel roads in Siberia.

Looking at Rocket Boy ONE in the train heading for Taiga station at the junction of this line with the Trans-Siberian mainline, I suddenly realised that he must have been tired. The five thousand kilometres we had covered together had been really hard. I felt a need to celebrate the achievement and cheer us up a bit. Perhaps the Siberian gods were willing Rocket Boy ONE and me to take a rest? Having come this far, I intended to at least enjoy the journey on the Siberian railway. (Happy thoughts drifted through my mind at that moment, before things got even worse.)

Crowds filled Taiga station where, after a light supper, I spread my sleeping mat out in the waiting room, and lay down. It wasn't long before a station guard came up and warned me that it was dangerous so I had better not sleep there. A moment later a couple of Pamiris started talking to me. They did not seem particularly aggressive or dangerous, but as I was concerned by what the station guard had said, I decided to move to another waiting room. The room was crowded but it was late and I was sleepy.

Tomorrow . . . Krasnoyarsk.

Even though I had to buy a whole rear wheel, the repairs could be done the following day. Considering the tight schedule I had I couldn't go as far as Irkutsk. As things stood at that point, I would probably only just make it across Russia without having to extend my visa. Even so I would be pushing it. There was no question that I would be able to get a visa extension, but I would still have to be careful to stick to my schedule every day. More haste, less speed. Hasten slowly.

I was looking at a girl wearing pyjamas with Doraemon printed on them, a Japanese comic character. The kindness of the people continued. The couple to one side of me helped me to unload my bike from the train and a kind lady to my other side helped me buy some *piroshki* (small Russian meat pies) The train was scheduled to leave at 3.15 a.m.

The old man in charge of the wagon stood at the door at the top of the steps and muttered, "Who's this Asian guy with a bike and a huge load? What a nuisance!"

This was no time to be treated like that. Not when I had such a big problem on my hands and needed support from anyone willing to give it. I was beginning to get genuinely worried that I would not make it to Krasnoyarsk without mishap. In the end the bald guy reluctantly helped me onto the train, where I found myself in a four-person compartment. Rocket Boy ONE ended up in his compartment (which I was grateful for).

I lifted my baggage on to the upper bunk in the darkness inside the compartment, trying not to disturb the other sleeping passengers, lay down, and was shaken into sleep.

As I was chewing bread for breakfast and staring at the countryside rolling by outside the train window, the door of the compartment opened and I saw the man from last night, and beside him another very skinny man. Judging from the look of servility on the face of the guard, I guessed that the thin man was his superior. Was he perhaps the chief guard? Anyway, the chief conductor, or whoever he was, raised an index finger and ordered me to come down and follow him. I was led to the conductor's compartment, where I was instructed to show him my passport and visa.

"This won't do," he said.

"What won't do?" I replied. "The other man let me on last night with no problems."

I looked at the bald man, expecting him to acknowledge what I had said, but he just stared blankly back at me.

"Sorry, but no. *Dengi, dengi* (We'll need some money, money)."

"Money? I paid at Kemerovo station. Look at the ticket. It says 144 roubles."

"Kemerovo is Kemerovo. Here is here."

The man was making no sense at all!

"Another thing – your passport says you can stay two months in Russia following the date you entered the country at Nausiki."

So, what was wrong with that? I was travelling on a proper visa.

"Give us 200 roubles anyway. Dollars are OK. Come on. If you don't pay up I'll have to throw your passport and visa out of the window. I'll hand you over to the police at the next station." At this he indicated that I would be handcuffed.

I was sure that they were taking advantage of the fact that I could not speak Russian . . .

"You've got ten minutes." The bald man opened the carriage window and stuck his left hand out of it clutching my passport and visa. His bloodshot eyes were cold, his face hard, and he didn't move a muscle. This bastard seemed to have carte blanche to do whatever he wanted. I'm not sure why I had left him in charge of Rocket Boy ONE. I had just about had enough. But this was Russia. Unless disputes were resolved with money, much more serious consequences could ensue. Feeling ridiculous, I resigned myself to coughing up. All I wanted to do was to get to Ireland.

"All right old man. You can have it. I've only got dollars though. How much in dollars?"

The thin man leafed desperately through a small notebook – 35 dollars. The stupid, skinny guy couldn't work it out. (It should have been 40 dollars.)

I suggested 30 dollars in my notebook, and Skinny nodded. So ended the negotiations. I thumped 30 dollars down on the table and left the compartment. Maggots! It had been ages since I had thought of anyone as a maggot. My anger gradually subsided, leaving me feeling a bit silly.

I was back in Krasnoyarsk after having travelled six hundred kilometres on a train journey that had lasted, with stops, a total of nineteen hours. The morning sunshine shone on the roof of the station, the return to Krasnoyarsk bringing nostalgia that warmed my relieved mind.

I phoned Valera, the young boy fluent in English, who said that he would immediately come and meet me at a bus stop not too far away. To get to the meeting point, however, meant a bus journey. I was moved by the generosity of the girl who helped me find the right bus, the old lady who checked where I had to get off with the driver, and the old man who helped me lift my heavy bike onto the bus. Their kindness reminded me of the other side of Russia and the Russians.

When I got to Valera's house, his mother, Larisa, was bustling around making preparations for a party to commemorate Valera's graduation from primary education. In spite of the fact that she was so busy, she still found time to look after me, running me a bath as well as preparing a meal for me. This was soothing therapy for a body and soul that had both suffered on the train journey there.

I lost no time in getting a taxi to the old bike shop. But there were no rims for mountain bikes. They were not prepared to give me a wheel from a new bike. Seeing how distraught I was (not that being upset made any difference), the moustached manager sat me down in a chair.

"Look, have some tea."

(Irkutsk . . .?)

I sat morosely there, deep in thought, for what must have been thirty minutes, when the 'big boss' (the shop owner I guessed), turned up.

"We'll take the back wheel off this guy's bike and put it on yours. 400 roubles, OK?"

There was no real question about it being OK. If they did not do the repairs there and then I would be simply unable to make a start. On top of that, the beaming face of the young owner of the wheel showed no doubt or hesitation. The price was a little high, but I was simply grateful to them for being able to do it at all.

The hub on the replacement wheel was exactly the same as mine, the rim was a Ritchey, and they fitted my gear set to the new wheel. They did all this for free. A thousand *spasivas* to you all!

Valera phoned to check train times for me, to be told that there was a train to Kemerovo that night. When I actually got to the ticket office at the station, however, I was told that all the seats had been sold and that I would have to wait for two days. My exasperated expression clearly indicated that this was no joke as far as I was concerned. The ticket sales woman said that there were seats on a train going to Taiga and if I was prepared to go there I could change trains to Kemerovo. Since this was the same route I had taken to get to Krasnoyarsk, it was fine but I was concerned about the connection at Taiga. It was a worry I would have to accept. A more significant problem was the fact that the train I would have to board left at five the next morning.

I decided to go to Marietta's place. I wanted to see them again.

Marietta was amazed to see me when she opened the front door. Nevertheless, the same smiling face showed how pleased she was. Chatting whilst I ate the light meal she had prepared, I felt I was home from home. Stanislav got up as I was on the point of creeping out at three thirty the next morning, and helped me with my baggage.

"*Schastlivo* (Go for it!)!"

They were such wonderful people. What would have happened to me if the Stanislav family had not been there?

"*Net, net, net!*"

It seemed there was no way the lady in charge of the passenger compartment wanted my bike in her carriage. She looked imperious. She took me to the other carriages, but the answer was the same, "*Net, net, net*". I had no idea why they were turning me away.

"It's OK by me. Come on," said the next superintendent we saw.

I put the bike in this carriage and stored my baggage

under a bed. The man in charge then came along and asked me to go with him.

"It'll be 120 roubles."

Not again! Give me a break. How about 100 roubles?

"O.K."

Later, the first woman I had dealt with came along and had words with the third man, to claim her slice of the action? Well, it didn't come to anything, which was good I suppose, but nothing could have been worse than travelling with my bike on the Trans-Siberian railway, not being able to speak Russian. I was not going to repeat the experience. When was the 'electric train' to Kemerovo? Whenever it was I didn't care. I was sick of trains. Back to Kemerovo, back to the hotel . . . it was all starting to get to me; my head was reeling and I was getting low on energy. Looking at the map I could see that from Taiga to Jurga and from there to Route M53 was more or less the same distance as from Kemerovo to the same point. My top priority was to compress my schedule so I decided to restart my journey from this spot.

And more important still was the fact that the sun shone and that it was calling to us.

The Pogues *Bright lights are calling me*
POGUE MAHONE

The road as expected was gravel but that was fine. The sun shone, warming my brow. I sensed the earth's vibrations coming through the saddle. The mosquitoes came out to play. Nothing could beat pedalling along when things were like this. I had no need for cars, trains, timetables, nasty maggot conductors or tickets.

"Oi, you. Stop!"

The face of a young man with a crew cut had popped out of the window on the passenger seat side of a white Lada and was calling out to me.

"You must be boiling. Here, have a drink of this."

Igor (the man with the crew cut), Pasha and Denis were offering me a drink of Danish beer. That evening (the sun was still high), about 10 kilometres from Jurga, my destination, a white Lada came towards me from the opposite direction. Enter Igor and company again. "Hotels are too expensive. Come to our house. You can eat with us." They had come all the way back just to invite me to come with them. Their faces showed nothing other than goodwill, so without a moment's doubt or hesitation I gratefully accepted the offer. *Spasiva.*

"The town's just over there, so you can put your bike on the roof of the car."

"*Net.*"

"Why not? It'll be all right."

"I'll cycle. I'm cycling the whole way," I explained, gesturing.

They ended up going ahead of me in the Lada all the way into town. Igor cheered me on the whole 10 kilometres, a drink of Pepsi in one hand.

The three of them were visiting Taiga in connection with their kitchenware business, and told me that they would have to take some documents to their boss.

Boss? What sort of corruption were they involved in? Were they mafia? The 'kitchenware' business sounded suspect to me. Igor seemed a nice enough guy but he had a mischievous air about him.

I let things take their course and ended up at the boss's house, only to discover that she was an attractive woman. Her husband, moreover, turned out to be a policeman. My fears proved to be groundless. To cut a long story short the boss and her husband seemed to like me and asked me if I would stay there. I enjoyed dinner with Olga (the boss), her English-speaking husband, Volodya and their quiet son, Vitalya. We had borscht, chicken thighs, potatoes, salad, home-made jam and none other than Camus brandy!

"Delicious! But not vodka!"

I was back on the road. I was back in the Russia I knew, the real Russia.

We drank until one in the morning. Suffering with a hangover and tired from the exertions of the last few days, I made a slow start the following morning. It was more than 170 kilometres to Novosibirsk, and at this pace I had my doubts about whether I would make it.

James McNally *Raglan Road*
EVERYBREATH

I had lunch at a café after about 120 kilometres and pedalled on from there, revived and in better spirits, under a bright, cloudless blue sky. Flowers of rape danced in the warm breeze. The dandelions had passed. We were drifting along together with the seasons. It felt good. I had *shashlik* after 150 kilometres. 20 kilometres further on it was time for a *morozhenoe* break.

Progress from there was rapid and in no time at all I was entering Novosibirsk.

When I saw the sign saying Novosibirsk, tears

unexpectedly welled in my eyes. Whilst I had been in pretty bad condition earlier and had struggled hard that day, I felt I had done really well over the past four days. Novosibirsk had been my mid-range target after leaving Irkutsk and in a way it had seemed quite close, but in fact I had not made it. It had been an agonising four days. Thinking about it then, I became quite emotional. Roads began to take off from the road I was on. We carried straight along the main road. In the middle distance, near where I could see some tall buildings, the road began to go downhill, and we shortly went under a tall railway bridge. The noise of the train passing high overhead brought back memories of the Trans-Siberian railway.

Emerging from under the bridge and reaching the top of the slope beyond, I was startled by a sign that came into view. It was a shamrock! What on earth was it doing there? And what was it for? Near the sign I came to a store and gasped in astonishment – The Shamrock Irish Pub, Novosibirsk.

Draft Guinness on tap right in the middle of Siberia. This was truly a miracle.

All I could think was that a reward for my having cycled this far had miraculously floated down to earth from heaven. I was saved. (It is believed that the closer you are to the Guinness brewery in Dublin, the fresher and hence more delicious the Guinness is. This is a fact. Novosibirsk was about half way between Osaka and Dublin and I can confirm the Novosibirsk Guinness is about twice as delicious as the Guinness in Osaka. I cycled there so I should know.)

Asked who he is by King Alcinous, Odysseus finally reveals his identity, and begins to tell the whole story of how he drifted across the sea and landed on those shores. First, he told of how, in the realms of the one-eyed Cyclops, many of his men were eaten by the giant, but, summoning up supernatural power, they pierced the giant's eye and escaped.

Elena and Anton

"O-machi shite imasu. Novosibirsk de wa watashi ga yorokonde o-tetsudai itashimasu."

("We've been waiting for you. I look forward to looking after you whilst you're in Novosibirsk.")

I was listening to fluent Japanese on the phone. My Russian friend Pecha had told me that Elena's Japanese was good before I left Japan. I felt close to Elena from the first time we spoke. She and her husband cared for me with heart-warming kindness in Novosibirsk. Elena came to meet me at my hotel as I had a lot of errands to do, as promised. Faxed (13 roubles a page), changed money at the bank, collected parcels from the post office (some post, including letters from friends had arrived safely!) and developed photographs; Elena, with faultless interpreting helped me get it all done without a hitch. She did it with a speed and dexterity that a lone traveller in Russia such as myself could only dream of. As a token of my appreciation I bought her a Guinness in the afternoon.

The great river Obi flows through the gigantic city of Novosibirsk. The large body of water feeding the Obi is the Novosibirsk or Ob Lake (known by locals as 'the sea'). Anton's family lived in Akademgorodok on the northern shores of the lake, in what is locally known as 'Science City'. About 20 minutes from Novosibirsk by train, Science City is home to a university and other educational and research facilities, and as such is one of Russia's academic centres. Elena explained that the city was world-famous. Anton's family lived there because Elena was doing research in archaeology (and acted as an interpreter several times a year) and Anton was teaching maths at the university. I spent a few enjoyable days with Anton's family in the peaceful 'Science City', surrounded by forests, taking the opportunity to update my journal, have my haircut, and do my laundry. The physical and mental exhaustion, which had been building up before I got to Novosibirsk, was alleviated. I owe them my deepest thanks.

I had several conversations with Ireland.

(Bridgestone Ireland)

'About the wheel failure, was it made by Bridgestone? I see. The wheel itself was made by another manufacturer. You've had no problem with Bridgestone components so please stress the point on the programme that you had a problem with the wheel but that it was made by someone else, not Bridgestone.

"I also gave Alva MacSherry of the Irish Times *this telephone number. She wrote an article about you, and this project got off the ground partly because of it. She feels a sense of responsibility and has been concerned that something might happen to you."*

The *Irish Times* telephone interview . . .

"What's the best thing that has happened so far? If there's more than one then that's fine."

"Doing it alone. . . the solitude? (Everyone's a friend)
Getting tired of it?
(Every day has its excitement)
The confidence to make it to Ireland?
(Of course!)."

The Gerry Ryan Show
"I had a haircut today, especially for the programme."
"It looks great, Yaz."

(On the subject of the Kemerovo incident and the maggot conductors)

"A station is a station. A train is a train. Mm, well that's very Russian. Very philosophical."
"You had a pint of Guinness? You can drink Guinness in the middle of Siberia? That's a miracle. Fantastic!"

"Tomorrow's wind will blow tomorrow."
When the time came to leave, Elena sent me away with words that I had forgotten and left behind in Japan. It was a wonderful expression, but fighting against the predominantly westerly winds as I had done every day, it was not easy to get sentimental over the wind. Blown along by these winds, nothing much happened. I just went straight ahead, concentrating, silent, at times half asleep, plugging resolutely onward, one pedal after another. I would get up in the morning, eat some bread and cheese in the tent, swallowing the food with drinking water on occasions to make it easier. Then I would pedal non-stop for about 30 kilometres. Sweets or a chocolate bar were staple mid-morning fare, then I would stop

for lunch after about 80 kilometres. I would also have many shorter breaks when I would drink some cheap juice from a 1.5 litre bottle bought at cafés. The 110 kilometre treat might be *morozhenoe*. After that I tended to take it a bit easier, setting up camp when I found a suitable location, and that was it. This pattern repeated itself, over and over.

Still, I needed to have something to focus on, a target. So I tried desperately to seek significance in even the smallest event. I made an effort to find the miraculous in minute, innocuous things. In that state of mind, the smiling face of an old man I saw earlier stayed with me until the evening. The voice of an old lady selling vegetables by the road, who cried out, '*Schastlivo*', 'Go on', echoed in the tent later that night. Each little incident lingered in the vacuum of the days that drifted by.

"Where are you heading?" said the driver of a truck as I studied the map in a café. "This is a good road if you're going to Omsk."

He drew a firm line across a roadless blank on the map with a biro.

The main M51 I was on turned sharply at Barabinsk, and started making what looked like a detour. He told me that I should go straight on at Barabinsk. The thick pen line, and the resolute look in the eye of the driver, suggested that perhaps I could rely on him and his advice about this 'new road'.

The Corrs *Forgiven, not forgotten*
FORGIVEN, NOT FORGOTTEN

Cycling on roads through swamps, I would frequently see flocks of crows and other birds. They flew very low overhead, and were often hit and flattened by speeding Ladas. I came across many corpses scattered along the road. Then there were my beloved mosquitoes. Squadrons of a size not hitherto seen attacked me in this damp stretch of country. We had quite a party out there.

A dark blue Toyota Carina stopped on the road ahead. A plump old man wearing sunglasses and his son got out. Seeing as how I was being bombarded by mosquitoes, the man gave me some Johnson's Insect Repellent cream, 'Off!'. Outdoor magazines had recommended it as being the most effective product, and I had searched for the cream in Japan without success. Here I was in Siberia being presented with some. I accepted the kind offer gratefully and applied the cream liberally all over myself. (The Off! works really well. I guarantee it.)

My 'Mr Johnson' also recommended this new, direct route. He drew the route in such detail that I could do nothing but believe him. About thirty minutes after he left, Mr Johnson did a U-turn and headed back. "I just heard on the radio that the temperature tonight could fall to zero," he said, and so I should take care. He had come all the way back just to tell me this.

The road and my body were in good condition the next morning. I made it to Barabinsk with hardly a break for 85 kilometres. I had maintained a respectable speed of 22km/h. A little later, in the middle of being showered with kisses by a small group of ladies enjoying a party at a café just outside town, I noticed out of the window that the rain had started.

A muddy battlefield

The main thing worrying me, and that everyone had warned me about, was an off-road section that began about 30 kilometres up ahead. It turned out to be like a battlefield, with big construction vehicles going up and down the road in the rain. It was fun to start with, having my picture taken with the labourers working on the off-road section, but the road had deteriorated to squidgy mud, sludge and slime. The main road itself was under construction and was impassable. This meant having to use this side road (hardly a 'road' at all), but in the rain it had turned into what seemed like a tilled and flooded rice field. Unable to morph into a tractor, neither Rocket Boy ONE, piled high with baggage, nor I, were going anywhere. The sticky mud clogged up my brakes. Accretions of mud grew like snowmen, so that in the end my rear brakes completely disappeared and were immobilised. I had to stop and scrape the mud off when the globs got to this stage. I was ready to drop, but I slogged on through the slime, until eventually it seemed that the mud hell was about to end. In fact the road became very greasy, and we both began to slide. We slipped over again and again. The earth was playing with us. It was a relief to eventually get back to our immediate goal, the asphalt road, but the day had been a wipe-out. We were both well plastered in mud.

'If at first you don't succeed, try and try again' was the proverb that stuck in my mind at such times. Rocket Boy ONE seemed to return to normal once the mud had been removed and he was clean once more. A thought then struck me. It was not we who were cycling around the world, but the world that was rolling around our wheels.

Japan is an overcrowded, cramped country, making it unpleasant in many respects. Nevertheless, there are many wonderful Japanese people. Rather than concentrating on Japan's weaknesses, I think I should approach Japanese people openly and honestly, and strive to understand them better. I must live my life with pride in the fact *that I, too, am Japanese. I had always thought this, but I was now more vividly aware of what it really meant.*

The hotel in Omsk refused my dollars. I tried everything. Without a moment's hesitation, the porter Alec suggested that I could stay at his 'No.2 House' for 100 roubles. It immediately struck me that this was about money again, but he did not seem the type, so on balance I decided that it had more to do with the fact that life was tough and he was just trying to make a living. I ended up staying for two nights. (In fact the 'No.2 House' turned out to be the home of Alec's grandmother who had passed away recently. It was rather eerie staying there.)

As it was a more direct route, I planned on going straight through Kazakhstan, although I did not have a formal visa. According to Alec, Kazakhstan was the same as Russia, so I would have no problem in crossing it – the roads were Russian after all. Rather than problems arising with my application before I departed, I had decided that I would not need one for the two days I would be there. Now, though, I started to become very worried about the lack of a visa. If I was denied entry it would mean my having to travel in a big detour northwards through Russian territory. If the worst came to the worst, I could be deported.

U2 *I Still Haven't Found What I'm Looking For*
THE JOSHUA TREE

My mother, my aunt, my younger brother's girlfriend, my Danish girlfriend Maria, Maria's family and my other friends, were going to turn out to meet me when I got to Ireland. How was I going to cope with all that? Perhaps it was too early to dwell on it. No, I felt it was okay for me to begin to start thinking about it now.

The intensity of the vacuum in which I seemed to be travelling was increasing. Now and then I found myself literally sleeping while pedalling.

The flat roads stretched endlessly ahead. There was no change in the landscape at all. No variation in the topography or the scenery. If anything, the silver birch trees might have been thinning out. By contrast, the flocks of black crows swelled to enormous numbers and many of them were hit by passing vehicles. In the emptiness that stretched for days on end, an endless succession of memories drifted through my mind.

. . . One early afternoon in Dublin I had my first experience of a real pub. There were five old men sitting at the bar. Their patiently brewed Guinness was lined up in front of them. But the men didn't touch the Guinness. They simply stared as the bubbles, forming a creamy head, sank lower and lower like a stage curtain falling.
Time drifted slowly by . . .

The Kazakhstan border lay just ahead. Rain. Would I make it across the border?

I had no difficulty at all. There was a checkpoint but the

only checks being done were on vehicles entering Russia. I slipped over the border without a hitch.

About 30 kilometres further on, there were big signs on either side of the road indicating the border. It felt less like a national border, more like a state or provincial border. The young man in a café I stopped at told me that Kazakhstanis spoke Kazakh and Russian. He insisted on my having some Russian vodka made in Kazakhstan (which he said had won first prize in a World Competition in 1961).

In a dream I had, my grandmother in Fukuoka made me some rice cakes with red bean jam inside. Before I set off the next morning, I checked my rear wheel and found that there was some lateral movement. The ring fastening the gears had worked loose. They had fitted it rather carelessly in Krasnoyarsk but I really needed to use the right tools for the job.

. . . I climbed Croagh Patrick in light rain and a strong wind. The man who gave me a lift there told me that Croagh Patrick was like Mount Fuji for the Japanese. I crawled up Saint Patrick's sacred mountain like a dog, frightened of being blown away by the gale. I was alone. Not a soul anywhere. I descended after admiring the magnificent view from the summit. Later, soaked to the skin, I went into the pub at the start of the walk and ordered an Irish coffee. The man in the pub said nothing. He put some sugar into a glass, poured in the whiskey in silence and then filled it up with coffee. He finished it off with whipped cream. Handing over the Irish coffee he said but one thing, "It's out of season for climbing the mountain . . ."

I arrived in Petropavlosk, the capital of Kazakhstan, under a clear blue sky. In a café on the outskirts of town I bumped into a sailor called Victor who told me he had just returned from the port of Toyama in northern Japan. He proudly showed me a Hokuriku Expressway map published by the Japan Highway Public Corporation.

The Achilles tendon on my left ankle began to hurt. I knew I had overused it. The 190 kilometres I had cycled on the day I made it to Omsk had been fatal. I would have to cycle carefully and nurse the painful tendon. The Achilles tendon was not about to tear, but I was afraid of causing major damage. Up ahead I could see a long queue of trucks. It looked like a border crossing point. Waiting in a queue like that you could literally be there until sundown. I decided to slip through looking as innocent as I could. The drivers were looking at me, but I just cycled along the queue, smiling back at them. I crossed the border the moment I knew I was in the inspector's blind spot.

I was back in Russia and could relax.

Van Morrison *I will be there*
SAINT DOMINIC'S PREVIEW

. . . The boat heading for the Aran Islands, a place I had long wanted to visit, pitched wildly. I forced myself to stand on the deck even though I was about to vomit. Soaked with spray from the waves I imagined that we were horsemen riding out to sea. Grey rocks covered Inishmore. Wherever I went I felt my heart being purified. The wind, the rain, the waves, the deafening roar at the precipitous cliffs at Dun Aengus,

153

*the smell of the grasses clinging to the rocks. Scoured
by the waves the hollow rumble of tumbling rocks on
the stony beaches. I felt cleansed to the very core.*
    Here was my sacred place . . .

A little insect had quietly attached itself to my arm whilst I
had been pedalling along. Look, I thought to myself, if you
hang on there to the bitter end, little insect, you'll end up in a
place you've never been before. You won't know anyone there.
You will be in a country with a strange environment and
different food. But it's your life. Do you have somewhere in
mind? Don't worry I won't brush you off. Stay as long as you
like.

Russian bus stops are great. They are painted in bright
patterns and liven up otherwise dull scenery. Inevitably,
perhaps I looked forward to seeing these bus stops that
appeared at intervals of about 20 or 30 kilometres. The real
masterpiece was an illustration of a family doing a Cossack
dance. The earth was green, but the sky was a shocking pink!
Talking of traffic. As I made my way along Russian roads I saw
many roadside graves. I know you can find such 'traffic accident
graves' even in Ireland, but the Russian ones are a bit special.
They have steering wheels on them, without any exception. The
steering wheels are taken from the crashed cars and moulded
into the roadside graves with a photograph of the victim. One
day I saw a big one with a huge steering wheel together with
more than 20 photos of victims. There must have been a bus
crash. The shower of rain beating on the tent stopped as
suddenly as it had started. Going outside, I saw a double
rainbow on the far shore of the lake travelling north. It looked
exactly like the rainbows I had seen in Clifden in Connemara.

I was singing the words to a song by one of my favourite Japanese rock bands – 'Hold on to your unfinished dreams'. The tears flooded down. This project had been my long-cherished dream. Once I had realised this dream, I was determined that I would embrace a new one.

Progressing swiftly along the level road, I suddenly arrived at Celyabinsk.

Looking at the clock tower in the main square I noticed that it was one hour behind the time I was on. So the time difference had been reduced by one more hour. I took pleasure in the knowledge that I was kicking down the time difference under my own steam.

Then the Ural Mountains appeared ahead of me.

Beyond them I would no longer be in Asia.

Celyabinsk, the last city in Asia

Lenin Avenue, Central Square. Old Russian timber houses were dotted here and there between the ugly concrete buildings. Celyabinsk was not particularly different to any other Russian city. It felt good being there, however, and the people looked happier, almost certainly because they reflected the strong emotions I was feeling about Celyabinsk being the last city in Asia.

We had finally arrived. It had taken about two and a half months to cover a distance just short of an amazing 7,000 kilometres, which meant that I had cycled across Asia at a slightly quicker pace than I thought I would. Above all I felt like saying "Well done" to myself and to Rocket Boy ONE. Both of us were beginning to show signs of wear and tear however. My left Achilles tendon was beginning to hurt badly. I had liberally applied muscular pain gel for sports injuries bought from a pharmacy I was taken to by a kind young man. But I was not sure if it helped. The pain kicked in whenever I started pedalling. Rocket Boy ONE was generally beginning to look tired too, but my most immediate concern was the loosening of the ring securing the gears on the rear wheel. I wondered whether a bike shop in Celyabinsk would have the special tool needed to tighten it. (I still regretted having left this tool out as part of an effort to keep my load down.)

I found one in a sports shop in town. It must be a rare thing in Russia, but there was store which actually stocked MTB tool kits. A young member of staff, Vlad, carried out a full service, including tightening up the ring and making fine adjustments to the gears. Watching him work he seemed unqualified to my untrained eye.

The whole job took about an hour but the young man stubbornly refused to accept any payment. *Spasiva, Bolshoi!* I bought a bottle cage as a modest token of thanks. Thanks to Vlad, Rocket Boy One was there in the hotel room later with me, gleaming, looking quite the thing. (I should perhaps mention that I always brought the bike into my hotel rooms in Russia. I was simply unable to relax unless I could keep an eye on him. If I lost my bike that would be the end of everything.)

My memories of Celyabinsk were mainly to do with the telephone calls I received. I got calls from all sorts of people congratulating me on completing the Asian leg of the journey. (The calls came through the hotel switchboard to my room.)

Gerry Ryan . . .
Well, make sure you cross the Urals safely. Then there will be Guinness. There are several Irish bars in Moscow.

Colm Conyngham, Bridgestone . . .
I know someone in PR at Guinness, so I'm asking her to organise a party for when you arrive. Guinness has been mentioned so many times on the programme that we'll have to include it somehow.

My professor, Someda . . .
What are the roads like? Are your visas OK? I wish I was your age. Anyway, don't drink too much.

My younger brother's girlfriend, Keiko . . .
I'm on my way to Ireland.
My granny and aunt . . .
Find your dream, won't you!

Ono . . .
(Ono had just opened a wine shop called Schatzkammer)
The first four days were good, but since then business has been slow. Have your feelings about life changed?'

Kii . . .
Toshiyuki Nishida (a Japanese actor) has just done a good programme about Mongolia.

My elder sister, Chie
How're you feeling?

Yasuyuki Ozeki

Mum
    They're saying that there's an 'unsanitary disease'
epidemic in Russia. That's what they're all saying in Japan.
Look after yourself, all right?
    (What on earth was this 'unsanitary' disease?)

Then finally from a woman on the internal phone . . .
    Sex?

    I successfully made my final post pick-up in Russia and
fitted the new slick tyres I had received to Rocket Boy ONE.
We were now in good shape for crossing the Urals and
pressing on into Europe.

5

Harasho, Russia!
Across the Urals to Europe

Leaving Celyabinsk I saw a road sign indicating the direction
of Moscow. I cannot describe my feelings at that point. Words
simply couldn't express how I felt about having pedalled this
far. Moscow was within range.

The Ural Mountains were now in my sights. Beyond them
lay Europe.

The earth began to rise and fall in a succession of ridges.
I was tired of the flatness of Siberia, and both Rocket Boy
ONE and I were chuckling with glee at this gentle wake-up
call. We weren't at all bothered by the light wind either.

Eleanor McEvoy *The Fire Overhead*
WHAT'S FOLLOWING ME?

The ridges gradually became bigger, however, and much
tougher. This was real pedalling. Serious cycling, which meant
pushing hard, struggling up steep hills, fighting your way up
inch by inch. Sweating hard, throat parched, it's tough but

there's no stopping. You have to force yourself to carry on up hills that seem to go on forever. 'C'mon, c'mon,' you mutter to yourself. Inevitably the hills go on. 'Oh, what! More?' you cry. Just when you thought you had reached the top of a pass, you realise it is just another curve in the road . . .

This was the spirit in which I climbed, descended, pedalled up, down, up, up, up, down, over and over again, when I noticed what looked like a cyclist approaching from the opposite direction. It turned out to be a middle-aged Dutchman called Gerald. He was unemployed but he had another job to go to. Whilst he was waiting he decided to do this bicycle trip. His route was from Holland through Eastern Europe to Moscow, then on to Irkutsk, Baikal, Ulan Ude back to Pelm by train and a little way to the south before heading back to Holland. It was a five-month trip. He had done a huge number of cycling tours within Europe and had prepared for this trip by studying Russian for about a year. How different to my preparation, drinking vodka in Japan instead of studying Russian.

Exchanging information about the roads we had both travelled, we sent our mutual good wishes to those we knew, directed our wheels in opposite directions and cycled on. It had been a chance meeting in the vastness of Siberia in one of the remotest corners of Asia.

All nations and peoples have their own standards or yardsticks by which they measure themselves and others. I always judged Japan and Ireland, their strengths and weaknesses, using my own criteria, but I realised I needed to be more open-minded and if I do make judgements to be more flexible.

"A bit further on, the gradient is pretty steep."

I didn't pay that much attention initially to what Gerald had said, given that he came from a pancake-flat country much of which lay below sea level. However it did become extremely steep. 100 kilometres further on I bought a litre of fuel, two litres of Sprite and a 500gram tin of meat for supper. Later I became more tired and the going got even tougher.

At just the right moment a lake appeared to my left and I made a beeline for it. The area near the lake turned out to be a great campsite. The air was full of birds whose cries echoed among the peaks of the surrounding Ural Mountains.

Before dinner, I decided to strip down to my underwear and take a swim to mark the watershed between Asia and Europe. Opening both eyes wide, the water I peered through was pale green and cloudy.

The pedalling Dutchmen

I had begun to see more and more pink flowers. Brilliant carpets of pink lay between the dark green forest trees on both sides of the road. The only flower and shrub names I knew were cherry, tulip and maple, so I decided to call these flowers *Asia saishubana* ('Last flowers in Asia'). It was as though they were forming a gateway of flowers leading us out of Asia. I could see a very large sign in the distance, at the very top of a hill. Cycling closer I saw that it was a 5-metre high sign, sitting on a solid foundation more than 2 metres high, supported by several metal posts.

'EUROPE'

Going around to the other side, it said

'ASIA'

Yasuyuki Ozeki

This, then, was the border between Asia and Europe.

Running right across the foundation, as if on a map, there was a thick red borderline. Placing one foot either side of the red line, I was a man literally bridging Asia and Europe. It was immeasurably satisfying. I had really made it to Europe.

The driver of a truck who was taking a picture of the monument with a Russian camera came over and spoke to me. "It's a hell of a road from here."

"Normal, normal." ('It's OK, OK.')

"By the way, have you seen the cyclists with beards?" He made a gesture indicating bear-like beards. "They told us they were from Holland."

I had met Gerald the day before, but he certainly hadn't had a beard then. He might have shaved it off, of course. As the driver had warned, the gradient suddenly became very steep indeed. It must have been about 6%. Up and downhill sections of about 7 kilometres followed one after the other. The terrain was a succession of big ridges, as one might expect in the Urals. Two cyclists appeared at about the 100 kilometre point, coming the other way. It was them, the 'bear-beards'. Stickers saying NL (Holland) were fixed to their loads. One of them, a young man called Ralph, had cycled the world, including the Karakorum. He was then on a round-the-world trip from Holland – Lithuania – Estonia – St Petersburg – Siberia – Magadan (Russian Far East) – Alaska – North and South America – Tierra del Fuego – Cape Town – Africa – Europe. He was planning to do it over two years, with returns home between the legs. Here was a world-class cyclist. He had sponsors who had provided his bike and panniers, and suppliers who had provided other fixtures and fittings. In exchange, he had to send regular reports to a Dutch newspaper. (When I told them about my sponsorship deals, they were amazed that all I had to do was to call in to a radio programme. On reflection I realise what a good deal I had.) An Internet site recorded their progress. The other bear-beard, Herbert, had neither sufficient time nor money, so was planning to circle Baikal, go to Ulan Ude, then get a plane home.

"We've had a following wind just about the whole way. It must have been tough for you."

The proud, bearded Dutchmen were right. It would have been much more enjoyable if I had started from the west. I could have zoomed along with the prevailing westerly winds behind me. But my goal was Ireland, and that was why I had cycled that way. There was no point in daydreaming about other options. We exchanged details and checked out each other's bicycles. A Czech cyclist whom the bearded Dutchmen had apparently come across a few days before turned up and the four of us raised a glass of Russian Guinness to 'bikers of the world'.

Half-joking, I said to the Dutchmen, "I met another Dutch cyclist yesterday. Dutchmen have always been described as the 'Flying Dutchmen'. Surely you're the 'Pedalling Dutchmen'?" In fact it seemed to me that there were Dutchmen cycling everywhere. There was the Dutch family I had met near Lake Baikal too. I had met very few other travellers on this journey at all, but I had repeatedly encountered Dutchmen in the saddle. Why such a high ratio? I wouldn't find out until I got to Holland. The Urals were truly where Asia and Europe met.

There is a Japanese saying about having your 'feet on the ground'. It has a similar meaning to 'down to earth' in English. Not being a particularly 'down to earth' sort of person, I had pedalled all this way in an effort to get my feet on the ground. Now it suddenly struck me that however much energy I expended in turning the pedals, the distance between the lower surface of the pedals and the ground remained constant. The vector, or downward effort to place my feet on the ground, simply resulted in forward movement. I wondered whether the forward vector and the downward pedal vector would tend to get fractionally closer and closer, and eventually cross at some point. If I stopped, of course, I could literally put my feet on the ground. But I was not going to stop.

Opening the flap and going outside, I found the site shrouded in dense morning mist, a clear reminder that I was in the mountains. The air was rich in oxygen that in some mysterious way seemed to permeate my body. I enjoyed a non-stop downhill ride from first thing in the morning and it felt like I was descending from a mountain peak and not just 10 or 20 kilometres. Notwithstanding the occasional slight rise, we're talking a distance of about 70 kilometres that flew past in the blink of an eye.

Carrying on swiftly over and down the mountains, we eventually emerged from the Urals. They had turned out to be a really broad mountain range. From start to finish, it had taken a full three gruelling days of pedalling.

Over the Urals, the trees and forested areas diminished sharply. In their place there were masses of colourful flowers. Houses of a different design to the ones I had seen in Siberia were dotted here and there across the wide open plains I was once again crossing. The houses and scenery began to look vaguely European. This might just have been me, though, excited at having crossed the Urals into Europe, imposing my pre-conceived notions on what I saw. Pedalling along with these thoughts drifting through my head, I was relieved to get to the city of Ufa. I was thinking what an incident-free day it had been, and was almost wishing something would happen when, crossing some tramlines, I heard a sinister cracking sound. A shiver ran down my spine. I wondered what the noise was. Had I run over something and broken it? I couldn't see anything. Something must have happened to the bike . . .

Carrying on I saw that the rear luggage rack was wobbling. Examining it more closely I found that the carrier was bent. I knew that it had a small crack, but I was hoping it would hold out. If it was going to break, then I had decided I would deal with it as and when it happened. What a pain!

Fortunately, there was what looked like a garage nearby. I barged in, only to be told, in no uncertain terms, "Tomorrow tomorrow." Seeing my plight, a kind young man took pity on me, and explained how I could get to another garage nearby. It was the same story there, "Tomorrow." The young guy in the garage told me about another workshop round the back. I asked them if they could weld the carrier, to be told by a man stripped to the waist, repairing a bus, "Tomorrow. The welding equipment is switched off at the moment."

What was I to do? All I could do was to wait until tomorrow. I shouldn't really have been that laid back bearing in mind my visa and my tight schedule. There again, apart from the Kemerovo incident, it was quite strange that nothing adverse had happened to me so far. I concluded that it might be sensible to devote tomorrow, just one day, to carrying out repairs properly, in an unhurried way . . .

Then I felt a hand on my shoulder. It was the young man, stripped down to the waist.

"Anyway, let's have a look, shall we?" The semi-naked Alexander ordered me to remove all my baggage. He checked the damaged area, rattled it around to see if it stayed in place, removed the bolts then took the carrier into the workshop.

The first thing he did was cut a little bit away from the damaged area. Then he secured a suitable bolt in a vice, and cut away both ends with a grinder. This bolt was fitted to the carrier and tapped into position with a hammer. He then skilfully secured the bolt with wire.

"Done."

He had used his brains – the wisdom of a Russian brought up with very limited resources and materials – and his kindness.

"*Spasiva*, Alexander. And Russian technology!"

"It'll get you to Moscow, even to London."

In retrospect, it was as if events had been waiting for us to get to Europe. In the days that followed the carrier bending and a number of other problems occurred in rapid succession. When they occurred, I had the defects welded and carried on. Reccurrence of the problems happened ONLY to those parts that had been welded. The area that supported the baggage firmly right to the end was the one that had been fixed by Alexander and his simple engineering.

Odysseus and his men received a warm welcome on the island of Aeolus, keeper of the winds. After a month, they started out safely on their return journey, but just as land was in sight, his followers opened the ox-hide bag in which Aeolus had bottled up all but the west wind, believing it to contain riches, only for a storm to be unleashed. The winds that had been released blew them back to the island of Aeolus.

Odysseus's men are transformed into pigs on Circe's island. Circe subsequently becomes enamoured of Odysseus, and he and his men spend one year there.

Beautiful Russian ladies

The Cranberries *Free to Decide*
TO THE FAITHFUL DEPARTED

I arrived in the town of Poisevo. As usual I looked for a café to have lunch.

I noticed a sign saying *Stolovaya*, meaning 'restaurant'. I didn't mind if it was a café or a *stolovaya*. I just wanted food! Rows of desks were lined up in the large, dim space and the smell of freshly baked bread and warm air filled the room.

"May I have something to eat?"

"Rees (rice)?" a lady asked me, with a broad smile.

The meal that arrived consisted of rice, steamed vegetables, beef soup (smelled like mutton), mashed potato, beef, bread and tea. They must have thought I looked starving and prepared the special menu for me. When I asked them the price, they told me it came to only 9 roubles.

"Wow!"

"*Daa.*"

One of the ladies came over to me whilst I was eating, "Would you like some more?"

She had a warm, amiable expression. I asked for more bread and tea.

"This bread is really delicious."

"I baked it here."

"Could I have a loaf to take back to my *palatka* (tent)?"

"*Daa.*"

About 5 minutes later, a second woman came over and handed me a warm loaf wrapped in paper. (Opening it up later, I found that the loaf had actually been sliced up for me. This explained why it had taken the woman some time to come back with it. How thoughtful!)

I asked how much all the food and bread came to.

'No problem.'

'Reall?'

It wasn't so much the issue of the money but that I was simply overwhelmed by the amazing generosity of these women.

Spasiva. Bolshoi!

We took a group photo and then I set off on my bike, cheered on by the voices of the women shouting "*Schastlivo* (Good luck)!"

As I came down a hill into the town of Naberezhny Chelny, a massive power station the size of a castle reared up ahead of me. Most likely a steam-generated power station, smoke was billowing from the chimneys on a scale so vast it seemed the plant was forcing up columns of cumulonimbus clouds. Long bundles of pipes went everywhere, to the left, to the right, over and under. The unbelievably big power station was located in the middle of a built-up area. Dangerous industries that might produce toxic fumes were obviously not located in remote places like in Japan. They stuck them right next to where they lived.

I supposed it meant savings in transporting energy, as well as reductions in labour costs. A community truly bound up in its fate.

Van Morrison *Sometimes We Cry*
THE HEALING GAME

The wind blew from the west again that day. The road was running in a west-south-westerly direction, which was OK. Even slightly stronger winds didn't concern me particularly now. I had been toughened by the predominantly west wind. If the wind was not head-on, it really didn't bother me that much any more.

Feeling a great distance between Ireland and Japan, the idea for this journey came to me as if I had been struck by lightning. I had wanted to think about what it really meant whilst pedalling across the Eurasian continent, the geographical manifestation of this gap. Thoughts about this had been turning over in my mind, bit by bit, slowly, and increasingly deeply, as I had covered the more than 7,000 kilometres. Now I was across the Urals and had entered Europe. What, I wondered, could I say to myself?

Did my dissatisfaction with so many things in Japan have something to do with my being typically Japanese? If I had had enough self-confidence, surely I would have come to accept things in Japan more readily? I had been looking at Japan with a cold, critical eye and so naturally had only tended to find things I did not like about the place. If I had approached Japan more sympathetically, perhaps more openly, I might have been able to see through those things I disliked and find the more valuable, worthier aspects I had overlooked. The one and only thing that had significance for me now was that I should live and die as a worthy Japanese person.

The more I pedal, the more I get to know the world isn't that bad. In the end every country has its good and bad points. The only significant differences are in lifestyles and cultures. When it comes down to it, we are all kind and wonderful under the skin. This planet isn't such a bad place. The only question, then, is which style is really 'me'?

The sky turned a cloudless blue for the first time in Russia. I noticed that the blueness of the Russian sky was comparable to that of the sky over Mongolia, but for some reason seemed a little less intense. I wondered what determines the blueness of the sky. Humidity? The sun's rays? The colours of the earth? Rivers? People's voices? Or perhaps it's the colour of our hearts.

Moved in Kazan

I anticipated the time difference to have diminished around then and as I checked into the Hotel Tatarsk in the centre of Kazan I learned from the girl on reception that it was now two hours less, so that we were already on Moscow time. I had pedalled all the way to the Moscow time zone under my own steam.

I talked to Colm Conyngham of Bridgestone Ireland on the phone. The Gerry Ryan show wanted to broadcast as much as possible following the end of the programme's holiday in August. There was a lot to be done including the planning for the reception on my arrival. They also planned to put many of my reports onto Gerry's home-page

They were planning a reception for me in Brussels, where Bridgestone Europe Head Office was located. They were also intending to contact Bridgestone Finland in Helsinki. Colm had also talked to people from Guinness and they seemed quite grateful to me. There had been a really long article in that week's *Irish Times* so I printed out the article at an Internet 'salon' in the town. The content was great, but it was really weird to be able to read an article, based on the interview I had done over the phone to Ireland in Novosibirsk here in Kazan. The world was shrinking and life was becoming easier and more convenient. Kazan was the capital of the Tartar Republic of the Russian Federation (or so the hotel staff had informed me) and walking through the streets I noticed there was a vaguely exotic smell. The people's features, the folk music in the streets, as well as the buildings had an Asian feel. It struck me as completely different to the Russian cities I had been through and it was a joy to walk around. According to my plan, I would reach Moscow in six days.

Odysseus travels to the Underworld, encountering all manner of ghosts: the spirit of his mother, his friends and other great heroes.

The great River Volga
About 40 kilometres from Kazan I reached the River Volga. So, was this the Volga I had studied in Geography? It really was huge. There were many boats, including pleasure craft, tugs, and fishing boats, going up and down the river. The water was very murky, possibly due to the recent rains.

Hot House Flowers *Good for you*
SONGS FOR THE RAIN

I wanted to draw a thin, but powerful, beam of light across the Eurasian continent. My next dream would be to look at this line, drawn on the earth, from outer space.

171

Yasuyuki Ozeki

Christy Moore *North and South of the River*
GRAFFITI TONGUE

120 kilometres on I reached the town of Borotinesh. At a shop just outside this rural town I bought yoghurt, bread, a tin of salmon and a cucumber from some ladies who wore broad smiles. That was quite enough to cheer me up. They continued to beam as they handed me some water. Outside the shop there was a stall where I asked for two potatoes. The lady there charged me nothing. The old lady at the next stall gave me a small bundle of dried fish (from the Volga?). The old lady next to her gave me two cucumbers. They were all offered as presents. *Spasiva. Bolshoi!*

As a token of my appreciation, I took a group photo with all of them. Asking them for their address, one old lady said 'the cost of a stamp!', and proceeded to give me another bundle of dried Volga fish. I had aimed to learn one Russian phrase every day after entering the country. Thanks to these ladies I had learned three that day. Because it was such a long journey I managed to learn a little Russian. The most important things, however, were the heart-to-heart conversations. At the end of the day, words were not essential. Putting up my tent in the rain, a lady with a basket full of mushrooms came over and started doing a twirling dance and singing Russian folk songs, then disappeared silently into the forest. She might have been a witch.

Now and then I noticed I was shedding skin. It was a lovely sensation.

Old skin would slip off my back and get caught up in the rear wheel. The rear wheel rotating turned it into fine fragments that were scattered into the sky behind me.

I had pushed it over the preceding two days, so that day I was taking it easy. It wasn't even four in the afternoon, but I was already at my destination for the day, the city of Nizhny Novgorod. A city almost in Moscow's backyard, it was very large and finding accommodation was an effort. Doing as I was told, I climbed to the top of a hill. At the top I found a monument with panoramic views. The great Volga flowed down below. The vast plain beyond the river shone in the sunshine, adding to the majesty of the scene. I think I can safely say that all great Russian cities have wonderful rivers flowing through them. The Angara River in Irkutsk. The Yenisey River in Krasnoyarsk. The Obi River in Novosibirsk . . .

The Volga, though, was the finest by far. I was looking at the river from a high vantage point, and it was probably the right season to see it in, but all things said and done, it had to be the most beautiful river in Russia. To my surprise and delight, there was a bar on the ground floor of the hotel selling draught Harp and Kilkenny. Moscow was close. I applied myself to drinking, fortifying myself for the three-day ride to Moscow. The Volga in the evening was even more beautiful. Some young local musicians were playing Russian music at an outdoor café. The only Russian music I had heard so far was Russian techno music in cafés. At last I could listen to some folk music. A golden sun sank below the Volga as I listened, transported by the Russian melodies.

I was alive in that moment. The trip was going so well thanks entirely to the many relationships I had formed and the kindness I had received, since I flew to Ireland on my promotional trip. One event sparked off another. To use a railway analogy, I had been guided by the tracks ahead of me since I was born. I had progressed by choosing certain lines, or having them chosen for me. Crossing a red light is likely to lead to an accident, so why not flip the switch oneself? Given that one must move ahead, why not change the lights oneself? Then again, I wouldn't want to get stuck on the JR (Japan Railways) Circle Line.

The Kolyas

"Is there anywhere I can put my tent up around here?" The smiling face of the old man in the evening sunshine was dazzling. "In the valley over there would be all right, but you could stay at my place if you like."

This was the holiday home of the Kolya family who lived in Moscow. To us, a 'holiday home' can mean many things. Mr Kolya announced, "This house is from Stalin's time." It had clearly seen many years of use. The walls leaned in various directions and the roof was patched. The floors creaked, but being Stalinist it had a certain style, and it felt peaceful. Mr Kolya's job had been growing wheat on a *kolhoz*, but he was now retired. There was his wife, Valya, their daughter, Galya, and her young nephew, the little Maxim. The cat, Muzyka. (I haven't mentioned them until now, but Russians are very fond of cats, and most of the families who looked after me had cats.) Everyone looked happy. It was a wonderful family.

They were growing large quantities of vegetables on their allotment, including tomatoes, cucumbers, onions, sweet corn, herbs and potatoes. There were chickens everywhere. Just about the only thing they needed to buy from a shop was bread. I was reminded of how well Russian self-sufficiency works. Mushrooms and berries gathered from the deep forest behind the house were piled high on a table in the garden.

Supper was soup made with one of their own freshly killed chickens. The fresh soup was flavoured with fresh herbs and lightly sautéed, fragrant wild mushrooms. Valya explained that these mushrooms were *apteka* (medicinal) *griby* (mushrooms). They popped up everywhere in Russia. Dessert was berries from the forest. It was a complete supper.

The Youth Olympics ceremony in Moscow was on the television. It looked like a big event and seeing it prompted Kolya to wonder whether I would be able to find a hotel room in Moscow. I felt most fortunate being offered hospitality like that in a family home. Having a delicious dinner and to be among such friendly people was really wonderful. I was delighted though I could hardly expect to be treated like that again before getting to Moscow. When I lay down on my creaking bed, Mr Kolya came in and told me, "Hashimoto. Prime minister of Japan retired on the 14th."

A puncture and vodka

Rattling along a bumpy asphalt road, head jolting violently I suddenly felt vibrations from the rear wheel stop and a split second later realised I had a puncture.

That had done it. This was the first puncture in Russia. In fact I had not had a puncture since about 400 kilometres short of Ulan Bator. This meant that I had not had a puncture for about 7,000 kilometres and more than two months. This was an almost miraculous record.

I recalled what Christine, the traveller I had met in Ulan Bator, had written on my helmet; 'Here's To No More Punctures!'. There must have been magic in those words. Although we were close to an area of housing, the surroundings were peaceful. I slid into my sleeping bag and started to think about arriving in Moscow the following day. I had come this far without any accidents or major illnesses and, though it might not be strictly accurate, thus far had avoided getting involved in any crime. I had, naturally enough, been concerned about potential incidents. Pecha had warned me about several things before I set off on my trip. He urged me to be careful about inflammation of the brain caused by insects such as mosquitoes in the forests of Russia, bears, wolves, other wild animals, and the dangers posed by that two-legged creature, humankind. The next day, however, I was going to be in Moscow. Either I had done well, or fortune had smiled on me.

A moment later I heard what sounded like a tractor in the distance. There was still some light left outside though it was already ten in the evening. The engine noise grew louder and louder. It seemed to be charging down on me. Had I been careless enough to erect my tent in a danger zone? Moscow was so close. The tractor pulled up just short of the tent. Had the time come, at last, for me to use the knife I always kept under my pillow? My hand gripping the knife was sticky with sweat.

"*Drug! Drug!!*"

(Friend? What friend? Don't try that one on me.)

I readied myself for the assault. Silently unzipping the tent inner, I opened the flap, then swiftly unzipped the flysheet.

No one there, no threatening faces, only a bottle of vodka looking back at me. Come on, guys, enough is enough. I'm tired. Being greeted by Russian farmers like this, though, I could hardly refuse. Well, why not, I thought in celebration of my puncture! So the three of us, the drunk Sergei, the sober ex-sailor Sergei and I polished off two bottles. It got later and later, but they showed no signs of going home, so I took a group photo of the three of us, and promised that I would send them copies. The two Sergeis at last got the message, and got up to go.

Returning from the Underworld, Odysseus finally sets off from Circe's island. He travels, by way of the sirens who sing to him, and Skyra, to the island of Trynakia. Having slaughtered cattle, which is forbidden, they encounter a storm where Odysseus loses all his men. Alone, he eventually reaches the island of Calypso. This ends his sea-borne journey.

To Red Square

Van Morrison *Too Long in Exile*
TOO LONG IN EXILE

I urged myself on. Pedalling hard generated considerable heat and speed. Cycling non-stop for about 60 kilometres, I averaged an amazing 23km/h. The urge to press on to Moscow and make it that day was unstoppable. Having said that, I was dirty and I stank. Entering Moscow in that state would have been most disrespectful. Since I planned to visit the Irish Embassy, I decided I would have to wash myself down and change into my Dinamo uniform.

But where on earth could I take a shower? Moscow wasn't a seaside resort, so there were almost certainly no shower cubicles, nor was I likely to find a clean river to plunge into. To my amazement I suddenly saw what looked like a shower sign! It was written in big letters. I had to just stop and check it out. I went around to the other side of the building, as directed by the sign, to find just the thing. A car-wash.

The young men running the place were as pleased to see me as I was thrilled to see their car wash. I urged them to indulge me by agreeing for a full wash down for both me and the bike! The sight of a grubby Japanese guy bent double going through a jet shower of a car wash with a bike must have been surreal. I felt completely refreshed after my car wash. A gleaming Rocket Boy ONE now sailed along in top shape.

We were now too excited to take in anything. Moscow gradually engulfed us. The buildings were taller than any I had seen in Russia, and pressed in on all sides. The number of cars, the speed of vehicles, and driver insanity were all of a distinctly higher order. We were sucked into the centre of the great metropolitan whirlpool, that famous landmark Red Square. We climbed numerous hills, crossed many bridges, waited at many lights and then I was sitting in the saddle in front of Saint Basil's Cathedral in Red Square, under a blue sky, smiling. I had pedalled 8,600 kilometres from Osaka.

Moscow diary
"Hang on a moment. I'll just fetch a map of the city."

The sumptuous room had queasily high ceilings and walls covered with highly valuable pictures. Bringing these features to my attention, Shane O'Neill, the First Secretary promptly left the ambassador's office and went next door. That left me alone in the ambassador's office wearing tee shirt and shorts. Nothing could have been more inappropriate.

"A pub in Moscow which serves good Guinness?" said the Secretary when he returned, studying a map. "The Shamrock Irish Pub on this street has pretty good Guinness but, mmm, it now lacks a certain appeal. So, although it's a bit far, the Sally O'Brien is good. It's a great pub. The Irish often go there . . ."

O'Neill, looking terribly serious, and with considerable dignity, then proceeded to give me a lengthy run down of the Irish pubs in Moscow. "If you want to check your email, you're quite welcome to use our computer." This was Kay, a member of staff at the embassy, who took me back to her house. A fine, slim woman, she never seemed to stop smiling. Her husband, Colin, greeted me at the house. He was English.

"First things first, have a shower."

('Am I really that smelly?' I wondered)

I had been touched by their kindness, but it suddenly dawned on me they were right. (In fact, my stinking shoes had already been banished to the verandah.)

Emerging from the shower I noticed that supper preparations were underway. It was a most enjoyable dinner enjoyed with Colin's mother. It seems she had arrived in Moscow only a day or two earlier. In the middle of the meal, Colin made a suggestion. "An Irish friend of mine, Danny, is manager of a big restaurant called Angara. There's a sushi bar there too. I'm going to ask Danny to treat you to a mountain of sushi." The next day rows of sushi appeared on the bar in front of me including salmon, prawn, eel, mackerel, salad roll, squid and salmon roe. Alongside there was *ikura* (salmon roe), incidentally, being a Russian word, tuna rolls, assorted *sashimi* and *miso* soup. To my surprise the *nigirizushi* were priced per piece!

The squid *nigiri* was exorbitantly expensive, but the quality of the fish in Russian fishmongers was generally pitiful, and the fish markets stank to high heaven. As Sõ had pointed out in Irkutsk, Russians did not eat much fish, 'Fish was for cats'. The land was so vast, one simply couldn't get hold of fresh fish. Which naturally explains why the fresh fish used for sushi was so expensive.

Danny, Colin, and Kay sat there smiling happily as they watched me eat my way through generous amounts of highly expensive sushi. I was so happy I could have cried. *Spasiva bolshoi* to the Irish sushi bar in Moscow!

The Guinness I had at the Shamrock Irish pub I went to later with Colin and Kay was twice as nice as the Guinness in Novosibirsk and four times as delicious as the Guinness in Osaka. The head was much, much finer. A road sign in the bar said 'Dublin 3,370km'.

I must mention the second occasion I was helped out by the Irish Embassy. I had been looking very hard for a bike shop that could do wheel alignment, but had so far failed. In the end, a Russian member of the embassy staff made exhaustive enquiries and eventually found one. On top of that, and to my embarrassment, I was driven to the bike shop in the suburbs in the absent ambassador's personal Jeep.

These people. What were they like?

The night before I left, Danny gave me a hip flask, and Colin filled it with Irish whiskey. "You can drink this only in an emergency. This is your last trump card – it'll get you safely to Dublin." Colin said this jokingly, but the thing that pleased me most was the message in the poem that they wrote for me:

May your journey be
As safe as a rock
As swift as the wind
As free as a bird
And make your heart
As big as the world

Colin and Kay *Moscow 20 July 1998*

Moscow surprises

I may have given the impression that all I did in Moscow was drink Guinness with the Irish. However I did the tourist thing too and spent as much time as I could walking around the city. Moscow covers a very large area, and has forests of tall buildings. The most surprising thing, however, is the Metro. The Moscow subway is incredibly deep. Escalators carry you down about 200 metres. It would be exhausting walking down, so all you can do is stand on the escalator. They move quickly but it took so long I almost yawned with boredom. Why are they so deep? The answer lies in the meandering Moscow river. The system was constructed by burrowing deep under the river about one hundred years ago. Other unforgettable aspects of the Moscow underground are the beautiful architecture and décor. It is just like walking through a museum with beautifully decorated windows, ceilings and pillars. It is also kept meticulously clean. The ladies who keep it clean work diligently round the clock.

Even more surprising was how low the fares were. However, the trains are comfortable. I really loved the Metro.

Telephone charges are also remarkably low. Colin told me that local calls from his house were free. Internet charges are also very low. Moscow rents average about 2,400 euro per month, thanks to the mafia. According to Slava, the ambassador's driver, all road signs had been in English until a few years earlier, but they had stopped using English because very few people understood them. Only the odd one remained here and there. The Kremlin was as imposing as I had imagined it would be. It was also very peaceful. The sort of hush that gave the impression something was moving around inside. When I started walking around Moscow the pain in my knees and Achilles tendon started to become increasingly severe. I wondered if they would be okay during the rest of the journey.

Tomorrow's wind will blow tomorrow . . .

Mary Black *Shine*
SHINE

Farewell Moscow

Taking care to avoid being hit by speeding rush-hour cars, the next thing I encountered as I left the great city of Moscow were lines of articulated lorries thundering along destroying any peace there might have been. Multi-coloured country stickers adorned the backs of the trucks travelling both ways. Finland appeared most commonly, then Sweden, Denmark, Estonia, Italy, Spain and Holland. There were trucks from Ireland too. This explained the wide variety of imported goods I had seen on the shelves in the Moscow shops and markets. Not only did the road signs giving distances have Russian numbers, they also displayed EU road numbers. The road I was on was the Russian M10 as well as being route EU95.

I saw many cyclists from the moment I hit this road. I was well within the European sphere here. I had entered the range of European travellers. There was no longer anything remarkable about me as a cyclist. I was simply one of many cyclists.

Aware of our situation, Rocket Boy ONE must have felt safer and more relaxed, because between Moscow and St Petersburg the bike had numerous mechanical problems.

Afternoon, July 21st

The strange sound I had heard before from the rear wheel occurred again here, so I checked it out whilst pedalling. Looking closely, I noticed that the chain was not quite engaging smoothly with the front gears, leaving it slightly adrift. As a result, the chain was rasping against the rear pulley. This was probably because the chain was stretching. It would have been all right if it was just stretching. If it broke, though, it would be the end. I just hoped it would last as far as St Petersburg or Helsinki.

I want to live my life in the way I choose, the way I feel.

Early morning, July 22nd

I had been aware of the rear tyre going down slowly since the day before. In fact it turned out to be a slow puncture. Inspecting the tube more closely, the 'easy patch' I had applied earlier had wrinkled up and slipped and air seemed to be leaking through a tiny hole. I had tried this kit because the instructions had said 'Rubber solution not required!' but it hardly seemed reliable. I replaced the tube with a spare and started pumping that up but as it filled there was a 'phssshhhh' sound. The hole was too big to use an easy patch. Air continued to escape after I tried repairing the puncture with a normal repair kit, so I stuck an easy patch on the first tyre and set off nervously.

My puncture repair kit supply had suddenly dwindled to just one easy patch repair set, so I decided I would have to buy replacements as soon as I could. I looked around several sports shops in Tober, the first town I came to, but none of them stocked a repair kit. I asked an old man selling fishing gear beside the road where I could find a sports shop selling repair kits, whereupon he led me to his house, and gave me a fragment of another tube and some rubber solution. He was proud of this solution and, understanding that this was the Russian way, I had no choice but to struggle on to St Petersburg with this repair.

"Money? Don't be silly. I just hope you'll make it."

He was clearly pleased to have helped. His kindness was warming.

It occurred to me that I had constantly been travelling on the very edge of the road. Reflecting on the received wisdom that 'Life is best lived on the middle path', it dawned on me that in fact, even if you live on the very edges, living life to the fullest is by far the best way.

The Pogues *Dirty Old Town*
RUM SODOMY AND THE LASH

Vividly coloured flowers brightened both sides of the

road. Looking at the now familiar scene of the Russians repairing their broken-down vehicles, I was certain that somehow or other I would manage. If Russians with their countermeasures were on hand to assist, we could fix whatever went wrong, even a broken chain. If I had a puncture, all cars and motorbikes carried tubes and if the worst came to the worst, I could always head into the nearest *shinomontazh* (garage doing vehicle repairs). This was simply the attitude people living in Russia had to dealing with problems. They had the skills and the tenacity of people who had little or no resources. I felt a deep respect and admiration for them.

To be strong, come hail or shine.

July 23rd

The noise of chain friction seems to have got worse.

The chain and gear meshing seemed to improve if I dropped into a lower gear, and the noise reduced a little . . . Like the Russians, perhaps I should simply have dealt with problems and repairs as and when they happened, but I decided it was sensible to pedal rather more cautiously than normal and not to push too hard.

Perhaps there was a message that I needed to listen to, a voice saying 'no need to overdo it. Simply apply feet to pedals and go with the flow'. The only alternative was to walk. In a sense my pedalling was dictated by heaven. Neither my knees nor my Achilles tendon were hurting and my average speed was as fast as 19km/h. This was O.K. because in the end I covered my target distance. At this rate I would just make it to St Petersburg, in spite of taking it easy.

Yasuyuki Ozeki

The Cranberries *Dreams*

EVERYBODY ELSE IS DOING IT, SO WHY CAN'T WE?

Huge numbers of watermelons had appeared for sale beside the road since before I got to Moscow, but there had been none since the truck of watermelons I had passed earlier. So long Russian summer of '98! Evening, at a roadside I bought three cucumbers, one carrot and one potato and all for one rouble. I only had a few more days left to be spoilt by such absurdly low Russian prices.

People, albeit unintentionally, seek 'absolutes' both in themselves and the things around them, but in fact everything is relative.

July 25th

I began to hear a creaking sound coming from the front wheel, about 30 kilometres after setting off. Checking the makeshift work I had done on the bolt mounting the previous day, I found to my dismay that the front carrier post itself had bent. It was an expensive carrier. Great! The cheaper rear carrier proved to be much stronger.

As shown on the map, the road going to St Petersburg was dead straight. There were neither cafés nor garages along the way. I eventually found a repair shop on the outskirts of a town called Tosno after having cycled about 90 kilometres.

Trying to convey my distress to the bearded mechanic, I pointed out that it was '*ploho* (cracked, rattling)! *ploho*!!'

"I can see that. Take off the rack and bring it in."

Enamel welding followed by surface finish sanding and hey presto, job done. He also welded the bolt mounting area.

"Money? Forget it."

The winds of change keep us moving forever onwards,
slowly, but surely.

July 28th

Pedalling cautiously along through St Petersburg, paying
attention to the chain, there was suddenly a twanging sound
from the front of the bike. This time it was the handlebar bag
carrier. I was horrified. What on earth was I going to do?
The frame was aluminium. If it had been steel I could have
had it welded, but as it was aluminium it needed a special
(argon) welding process. Would they have such facilities here? I
asked loads of people, tried many shops, and wandered many
kilometres.

About to give up in the rain, I stumbled across a repair
shop somewhere on the outskirts of town. They had no
argon welding equipment there, but the young man, who at
a glance I felt I could trust, told me that there was a repair
shop that could do argon welding in the suburbs. To my
surprise, he said that a friend of his had to go over there on
business, and that he could give me a lift. Looking at him I
decided I had nothing to worry about, and hopped into the
car without even bothering to lock the bike. The argon
welding was done without any problems. Asking how much it
cost, the old mechanic dismissed it, giving me a 'No need for
any money' kind of face. To settle the matter, he asked me to
pay 10 roubles. It was nowhere near enough of course. The
same day I finally found a Shimano IG chain in a specialist
bike shop. At 208 roubles for the set, it was four times the
price in Japan. No doubt the price had been hiked so high

because in Russia parts like this were toys for the rich and there was no demand. I had no choice but to buy one.

Anyway, how could I complain when the two young men in the shop worked so hard to change the chain, then, as usual, charged me nothing for the labour? (My old chain, incidentally, had stretched by about 5 links. This was to be expected, given the friction over 9,000 kilometres.)

For the first time in a long time I got the front and rear sets into top gear and found myself pedalling along as hard as I could. It felt really good. No problems.

The streets of Raskolnikov

St Petersburg, 'Venice of the North', was beautiful, deeply, refreshingly beautiful. It was good to walk around. The absence of the sort of stress I felt in Moscow had everything to do with the relaxed nature of the city. As Colin had pointed out, the city had a much more European feel to it, and was just like an old capital.

My first impression on the day I arrived in St Petersburg was how peaceful the city was. There was the sort of hush you might expect if a monarch (if there had been such a person) had just died, and the whole town was cloaked in mourning. Perhaps I was just comparing it with Moscow. It lacked Moscow's rough edge.

Walking around the city at daybreak I still felt settled and peaceful.

Gilding the sophisticated, serene city of St Petersburg was the great river Neva. The beautiful rows of buildings seen from a sightseeing boat . . . Draught Guinness on sale at the pier . . .the city spreading away from the south bank of the Neva forges an intimate fusion of history and refinement.

Beautiful canals flow through the city. The sphinx statues at the Bankovskiy Bridge, the Hermitage Museum, the large number of fine art collections, the Egyptian mummies and Van Gogh left me feeling dizzy. Further out, smiling Russian faces glinted at a naval festival. The Church of the Resurrection shone under the deep blue sky. The *matryoshka* dolls modelled on Yeltsin stood for sale at the souvenir shop in front of the churches. The sculptures in the Summer Gardens were fragrant with the scents of summer. A succession of brides and grooms passed through the gardens. I bought a photograph of a boy on a bike from young, local photographers, Marina and Cyril. The city's Metro system ran deeper than the Moscow Metro. Sparklingly clean with a big, lively central market. It reminded me of the Irkutsk central market. Thinking of things back then made me realise how far I had come and of all the Russian food that had passed through my tummy. Colourful restaurants dotted around town and I drank Baltika beer with a young couple at a terrace café. That girl was gorgeous. It was truly a city to visit with your boyfriend or girlfriend.

Do svidaniya, Russia

The Saw Doctors *Never Mind The Strangers*
ALL THE WAY FROM TUAM

I was going up quite a steep incline in light rain. Finland, which had been signposted, was steadily getting closer. I felt happy and sad at the same time. Should I call it a day and turn back? My time there and the distances covered in Russia had been considerable. I had accumulated many memories and warmed to Russia. If it weren't for Ireland, I would dearly have loved to spend more time travelling around the country. I so wanted to meet more Russians. There would be no more cafés from here on. No more old boys in cafés. No more *pelmeni*, no more *borscht,* and no more *hyper-shashlik.* I could no longer eat tasty *morozhenoe* for my snack break. No more listening to Russian techno. *Atkuda. Priama, Priama. Schastlivo! Davai! Davai!* I would no longer hear these exhortations either.

Mad Lada drivers would no longer fly past me and there would be no more wide open plains, fiery vodka and infinitely kind and homely Russians . . .

The next moment the border post sucked us in.

Spasiva Bolshoi Russia! Until we meet again, *do svidaniya!*

I heard a voice somewhere say *'Pozhaluista'* ('Don't mention it').

6

Nibbling at Europe

When, after crossing the border, I saw the EU circle of stars symbol, I lost my head and raised both fists in triumph. As well as feeling satisfied and elated at having made it all the way to Europe, I felt relieved at having made it safely to a more 'civilised' part of the world. The moment I left the border post the 'civilised' part of the world opened quietly ahead of me. Drivers observed the speed limit and drove in a much calmer way. (It was obvious who the Russian drivers were by their aggressive overtaking.) Painted homes glistened and the lawns looked neat and tidy. (In Russia they just let them grow.) Everyone I asked directions from – people on the road, women in the supermarkets, an old grocer – spoke perfect English. The supermarkets, which stocked everything, were clean, but that was hardly compensation for the price tags.

Travelling from Russia to Scandinavia was a major shift. While it may be huge there is no way you could flatter Russia by calling it an 'advanced' country. On the other hand, the countries of Scandinavia, including Finland, are arguably the most advanced in the world. The border may only be a few kilometres long, but crossing it means crossing a cultural gulf many hundreds of kilometres wide. The difference was startling. The cycle tracks, separated by a small distance from the road, were well maintained. They were more or less equivalent to Russian A roads. The cycling was excellent. I was able to pedal safely along without worrying about the proximity of passing cars.

However I felt something was missing. Although the Ladas flying along had been dangerous, I felt nostalgic for cycling in Russia. It had at least been stimulating. The painted homes, the lawns, and the perfect English here, all seemed rather superficial.

Welcome to Helsinki

I dropped in on him unannounced, but Mr Brennan, the cultural attaché at the Irish Embassy, greeted me with a smile. He listened to my story with deep interest, then gave me detailed information about accommodation and the ferry timetables.

"When you get to Dublin, make sure that the very next thing you do is tour round Ireland." He presented me with a guide to cycling in Ireland.

As arranged, the Bridgestone Finland General Manager, Mr Tähtinen, was waiting at a terrace café in front of a statue by the harbour. With Tähtinen were the Marketing Manager, Sari, and Tähtinen's handsome young assistant, Toni. Tähtinen had a camera and video with him. A flag saying 'Formula 1 The Challenge' fluttered on the table.

We were ushered into a splendid hotel facing the harbour, where we celebrated my arrival in an indoor terrace restaurant. The starter was a variety of fish and shellfish, including smoked salmon and sill (smoked herring). The main course was grilled almond salmon and the Petit Chablis went very nicely with our meal. The Baltic Sea stretched away into the distance. It was absolutely heavenly.

(Was it really all right for me, in my shorts and tee shirt and in my smelly and grubby state to be eating such a splendid meal in a place like this?)

Aware of my accommodation situation, Tähtinen suggested, "If you've nowhere to stay, why not stop over at Toni's tonight?"

I was surprised and grateful at this further offer of hospitality. "And Bridgestone Finland would like to buy your ferry ticket to Stockholm tomorrow as a present. I assume a single room with a shower would be acceptable?" Making the booking on his mobile, Tähtinen chuckled repeating, "In return, make sure you fly the flag for Bridgestone in Ireland."

Cute trams trundle busily along the hilly city streets. Indeed they would have looked at home in a theme park. The candlelight, spilling out from café windows, was the main source of light on the city streets at night. Fishmongers packed the central market in the morning. Salmon and more salmon . . . Fish glinted in the sun, sardines, trout, lobster, shellfish and all manner of shrimps and prawns. The sea harvest radiated freshness. I had not seen fresh fish like that since visiting the Kuromon market in Osaka before I left Japan. You could also buy fresh fish from the small boats lined up along the harbour. This was literally fresh seafood delivered to your door. It was to be Helsinki's turn to be the European Capital of Culture in two years' time. I noted the building sites around the city centre. To avoid ruining the city's appearance, images of buildings that could easily have been mistaken for the real thing were printed on the noise prevention screens that covered buildings under construction. Crossing to one of the islands, known as the 'Gibraltar of the Baltic', I saw the remains of an old fortress. The 'p' sound is extremely common in Finnish and gives a characteristic 'bouncy' feel to the language. In the small but rather pretty underground, the carriages were a fresh orange colour, though I found the plastic seats a bit chilly. The escalators were long, but they were nothing compared to the escalators of St Petersburg . . .

Kiitos, Finland

The icing on the cake of my enjoyable two-day visit to Helsinki was the boat trip to Stockholm, a present from Bridgestone Finland. The ferry itself was fantastic. The boat, the Silja Serenade, is extraordinarily tall, so I got a sweeping view of Helsinki below, from the deck. It was luxurious inside with seven restaurants, six bars and an enormous promenade. It also had a big duty-free shop. It looked just like a floating luxury hotel. What a splendid way to be transported to a neighbouring country for the weekend! This was real Scandinavian style. The room I was allotted was a fine one too. It was on the eleventh floor and was reached by elevator. Being on the top floor, I assumed it was one of the best rooms. A single room with a shower, I could look out of the window and see the bustling promenade below. It must have been expensive. I wondered whether it was really okay to accept such generosity.

Seeing as the whole boat journey was a present, I decided I would indulge myself and have a good dinner. I attacked the

RUSSIAN GENEROSITY • These market women stocked up my
food store and refused to let me pay

MORE RUSSIAN GENEROSITY • The Kolya family. They insisted I
stay with them in their house from Stalin's time.

RUSSIA • Where Europe and Asia meet

MOSCOW • Red Square

RUSSIA • The Pedalling Dutchmen

FINLAND • Crossing a cultural gulf

EUROPE • Blown away in Holland

HOLLAND • Heaven – A typical rocky Dutch road!

GERMANY • Harvest festival style

IRELAND • Victorious arrival at St James's Gate

IRELAND • Fame at last – meeting Gerry Ryan

IRELAND • Time stands still again – a pint of plain

Serenade Buffet with gusto, eating my fill of a wide variety and large quantity of the delicious-looking Baltic goodies. Naturally, I ordered a bottle of good white wine to complement the food.

I was sitting at the same table as a Finnish family – the husband, Tapani, who smiled at me politely, his sociable and charming wife, Sinikka, and their three children. We had a long chat and when I finally got round to asking the waiter for the bill, he said

"This gentleman has already paid." I looked at Tapani in surprise. Sinikka immediately explained, "We enjoyed dinner so much this evening. We really appreciated talking to you and hearing all about your adventures. The dinner is a present from Finland, celebrating your successes so far and wishing you good luck for the rest of the journey." It seemed that everyone was sponsoring me.

Kiitos. Paljon! (Deepest thanks)

Christy Moore *The Voyage*
VOYAGE

The Silja Serenade sailed southwest through the Baltic Sea, passing many small islands along the way. The clear, softly glowing Finnish sunlight turned the sea ahead of us gold as it sank into the depths.

Sweden, a sophisticated nation
"What a bizarre beard! You look like some sort of Asian swindler."

I had covered 9,800 kilometres, and it had been nearly four months, since I left in April. A year had passed since we said our farewells at Copenhagen airport. I had not idled the time away that year though and thoughts of Stockholm and meeting up again with my Danish girlfriend, Maria, had been constantly in my mind. Since setting out, not only had I tried to see how long I could grow my moustache and beard, but had also been wondering about what it would look like at our reunion. I wasted most of the day knocking about Stockholm. Four o'clock arrived at last and I waited, as arranged, in front of the Tourist Information Office at the Central Station. The moment I caught sight of Maria with her bike, my emotions overwhelmed me. I embraced her but being so flustered, those first words she uttered went straight over my head.

That night, Maria shaved off my beard, leaving my face as smooth as a baby's bottom. The cycling trip through Sweden with Maria proved to be refreshing, sweet and full of joy at having a smooth face again. The weather was kind. It hardly rained on us at all. As the reader is unlikely to be that interested in my amorous recollections, I will not go on about them for fear of your giving up and putting the book to one side. Instead, I will give a snapshot of what happened on the journey through Sweden.

Stockholm was much bigger than I expected. The buildings were breathtaking and although grand they looked just perfect in their settings. There were up-market streets in the old town. Colourful flags fluttered on the masts of yachts from many different countries that lay in the spacious harbour. The magnificent Vasa Museum, the Sunday market in the central square, the line of household cavalry sporting fresh blue uniforms as they trotted by on the road, the trains and the buses. Wherever we went, I was deeply impressed at how clean and bright everything looked.

Most towns and cities in Sweden I cycled through were as attractive in their own ways as Stockholm. The wilderness lies on Stockholm's doorstep and the Swedes live in harmony with nature. The environment is so fresh I could almost see the oxygen being pumped out by the endless expanses of forest. The days are long during Scandinavian summers. The lakes that stud the landscape are like myriad stars reflecting the sunlight absorbed until late into the evening. The earth looks a bit like a mirror ball. The land is laced with large and small rivers. All things glittered in the firmament: people, clouds, cows, sheep, foxes, horses, deer, wild rabbits and fish . . .

Swedes lovingly conserve nature. Entry to nature conservation areas is forbidden and rubbish for recycling is separated into six different types of container. It is large, but how a country with such large-scale industry as Sweden can conserve nature so assiduously and effectively, remains a mystery.

There is one image of the scenery in Sweden that sticks in my mind. It is not of the forests, the lakeshores, or the riversides; it is of the capital, Stockholm. Walking along a waterfront in the city one evening, we saw an old man just walking along, trailing a rod in the water. He said he was fishing for salmon. In fact he caught quite a few. Being able to catch salmon like that in the very heart of a city was another reminder of how civilised a society it was and how high the quality of life was there.

Well-planned and maintained cycle tracks run everywhere across the countryside. Paved cycle-ways stretched in a systematic way with hardly a pothole, from the suburbs into a countryside where there were unpaved tracks. It was brilliant cycling.

The campsites were good too. In Sweden, land is generally regarded as publicly owned, so we could camp where we liked. In so far as there were no signs saying 'Private land', we could pitch a tent anywhere, be it by the road, opposite someone's house or even on a beautiful site next to canal lock gates. In a way it was similar to Russia, but being in a more advanced country made the freedom of access that much more special. The campsites dotted here and there had good facilities and provided for all our needs. Sweden, I concluded, must be the place where you had to come if you wanted to experience nature to the full. From time to time as I pedalled along I came across long straight stretches of road with an excessive number of lanes. I learned that these could and would be used by fighter planes for taking off and landing, if there was a war. A country obviously not affiliated to NATO. Taxes, on the other hand in Sweden are sky-high. The levying of high taxes is the price paid for living in such a perfect country. Looking at the prices in supermarkets made my head spin. Commodity tax was about 25%. This made a 500cc bottle of Coke 2 euro and an ice cream 1 euro. Income tax can be as high as 50%. This was severe, but as the revenue from taxation is effectively targeted at health, the elderly, education and other services and sectors of society, it seemed justifiable.

Still, these taxes were harsh on the traveller. I must mention the alcohol situation.

Basically, supermarkets can sell drink only with an alcohol content of 3.5% or less. The alcohol you can buy in supermarkets is predominantly low alcohol beers and cider that you only start to feel mildly tipsy on after about 1.5 litres.

Can the Swedish not drink wine? Of course, they can, but they can purchase it only from chemists (and you will only find it in these or similar stores). So booze is treated in the same way as medicines. Hardly the stuff of romance or excitement, I thought. I sympathised with the Swedes and wished people were not controlled by the state like that.

The Gerry Ryan Show, again

As though waiting for me to get to Sweden, the Gerry Ryan Show was back on air after a four-week holiday. (From a café in the beautiful harbour town of Västervik:)

"Long time, Yaz. Glad to hear everything's OK. Where are you now?"

"Well, a man is baking a pizza next to me."

(At a petrol station outside the town of Höör)

"Where are you today?"

"A woman is grilling a hamburger next to me."

The Commitments *Destination Anywhere*
THE COMMITMENTS

Maria and I arrived in the port city of Malmö on the south-western tip of Sweden after ten enjoyable days of cycling. My heart missed a beat, however, when I set eyes on the high-speed ferry terminus. Every day since leaving Osaka had brought new vistas. Here, after all that time, I was about to set eyes on a place I had seen before.

Long time no see, Denmark

The high-speed boat arrived in the pretty little harbour of Nyhavn. The scenery along both sides of the road from there

Yasuyuki Ozeki

to Maria's flat was all so nostalgic. The sausage stands, the pizza house, the furniture shop, the Greek restaurant, Nørreport Station, the kebab shop, the pond, the supermarket, the chemist, even the greengrocer. Everything was nostalgic, from the crossroads on the street with a kink in it to the smell of the city. I felt Copenhagen in my bones. I was at last reunited with my memories, with experiences I'd had there.

Summer in Denmark is neither hot nor cold but it is refreshing. What struck me was how lively the faces of the people were. This was the first time I had seen them in summer. They were completely different to their winter faces. I was stunned also by how beautiful the women looked. The colour of the roads, the sound of the leaves in the trees lining the streets, the songs of the birds, Tivoli Park blossoming in the summer light; everything was so fresh it made winter Denmark seem like another country altogether.

The Irish Embassy and Bridgestone Denmark
"There was a fax from Ms Egan in Tokyo. Everyone here knows about you."

I was greeted by the First Secretary, Eamon, sporting a fine set of sideburns. Eamon had taken up his post in Denmark two weeks earlier and his desk was covered with housing guides, school information and other pamphlets.

"Take this CD and listen to it whilst you're cycling along to make you think of Ireland." He gave a deep, soft chuckle as he presented me with the CD.

Carl Hession – *Old Time New Time*

200

I also got a fantastic welcome from Bridgestone Denmark. "A present from Bridgestone Denmark, to celebrate your birthday and your having cycled this far."

This was Tony speaking to me. He is head of business operations on the Copenhagen island of Zealand. He handed me a gorgeous bunch of flowers and the first one thousand Krone note I had seen. "Perhaps you could enjoy a delicious meal with your girlfriend?" They arranged a meeting with a journalist from a motoring magazine. The interview lasted for about an hour. "*Tusind tak* (Thank you very much), Tony!"

What characterises a so-called 'great' country? A high-speed road network and exhaust fumes? Cheap alcohol? Luxury cars? Massive farms? High-rise buildings? Architecture oozing history or speed signs for military vehicles?

The moment I crossed the maritime border into Germany by ferry, I was greeted by the shapes, the air and the speed associated with a 'great' country.

Something's missing

It was good having the sort of security provided by cycle tracks that were fully integrated into road networks. However, pedalling along those tracks against oncoming streams of cyclists, I became even more aware that I was no longer special – I had returned to being a face in a crowd. When asked by neighbouring campers where I came from, I answered, "Japan". Seeing the half-interested responses to that, I added that in fact I had undertaken the entire journey under my own steam. This would throw them completely, as if they had misheard, lost the thread of what was being said and decided to give up on this line of enquiry. The conversations I had invariably followed this pattern. Perhaps they didn't believe my story. Perhaps because Japan and Europe were so closely linked by air, there were many Japanese cyclists drifting around this part of the world on their bicycles.

At these times I felt a longing for the times I spent in Russia. I might have battled against Ladas, but at least I had the Russians encouraging me to cycle on.

Christy Moore *Before the Deluge*
KING PUCK

I was now in the suburbs of Hamburg. I stupidly forced myself to continue pedalling on through the interminable rain. I had asked the way but later discovered to my dismay that the road I was cycling along in the direction of Bremen was an autobahn.

I was drenched by the spray and deafened by the scream of horns from Mercedes and BMW cars as they sped past. Were they telling me to get off the road? I wanted to get off it but there were no exits. All I could do was battle on to the next exit . . .

In the end, a big articulated truck came up behind me as I cycled along the hard shoulder and began honking its horn so loud I thought my ear-drums would explode. I had no choice but to stop. The truck pulled up too and the driver jumped down from the cabin.

"This is an autobahn. You know that cyclists are not supposed to be here I suppose?"

"I realise that. But there aren't any exits, are there?"

"You'd better get down onto the side road."

"I can see the side road, but the guard-rail is too high. There's no way I can get over that."

"Why not?"

"Why? Look at that load! I wouldn't get that over."

So the conversation continued in the pouring rain until, without a word, the driver lifted Rocket Boy ONE over to the other side of the guard-rail.

"Danke schön!"

Police chase

The second I dropped down onto the side road I heard the siren of a police car approaching and stopping right above me. (Reckless, reckless. The police could have arrested me! Someone must have informed them. What would have happened, I wondered, if the lorry driver had not been there to help? Anyway, I thought, I'd escaped this time.) Pedalling along, happy to be off the autobahn, I was about a kilometre down the road when I saw a stationary patrol car up ahead with blue lights revolving on the roof. They must have turned off the autobahn up ahead. I couldn't bear it! "We've had a report from a driver." Slanting rain lashed the face of the lean, mean-looking police officer. "That's an autobahn over there. Do you understand? It's a highway?" (That was it. I couldn't take any more. I was beyond coming up with excuses.) "Cycling on autobahns is forbidden." I stood there silently, staring at the lean officer.

"Where have you come from?"

"Japan."

"By bike?"

"Yes."

"What, the whole way?"

"Yes."

Mr Lean was obviously gob-smacked.

"So where are you heading for now?"

"Ireland."

"Ireland? Why Ireland?"

Strange question.

"Why? Well . . . yeah, I like Ireland."

His face was assuming an increasingly improbable expression, when a voice came over his radio. Mr Lean got back into his patrol car. "Well, all the best!" The patrol car disappeared into the rain like a puff of smoke.

Holland – bicycle heaven

Perhaps it was just my imagination, but the moment I crossed the border the land seemed to become as flat as a pancake. Even if it was something I had read about before in textbooks, it was immediately obvious. An irrefutable topological reality unrolled ahead of my tyres with no apparent end. Yet there was something that was more obvious and which held much more significance for me, than the land simply being flat. Namely the fact that the cycle track network was perfection itself.

The cycle tracks were so well maintained. In nature conservation areas, the asphalt cycle track surfaces were stripped away. Instead, the soil was flattened to make a cycling surface. This was more environmentally sensitive than asphalt. The Dutch clearly paid careful attention to the natural environment. Expanding the areas covered by cycle routes had resulted in a complete network of tracks. The most amazing aspect was the special signage used along the cycle tracks. Not only did the signs show where you were going, they also indicated exact distances. The distances appeared on all the signs, not just on the odd one! Cycle tracks are generally quite good in continental Europe, but in Holland they are exceptional. How could the Dutch not love cycling with tracks like that? Every day I encountered riders coming the other way. I overtook riders and riders overtook me. Old people, young people, men and women, tall people and little people, the poor and the rich. There were all sorts of bikes, from those you seemed to pedal standing up to recumbents where you almost lay down. There were bikes with small auxiliary motors for the elderly, unicycles (!), tricycles, tandems, bikes with big carriers and parent-and-child bikes. There were people with all manner of wheels cycling everywhere. At last I understood where the guys I had met earlier on my trip were coming from. I finally understood the sentiments of the Dutch mother and child I had met at Lake Baikal, Gerald, the middle-aged Dutchman I had seen in the Urals and the bearded Dutchmen. Growing up in a place like that, you would use a bike every day and cover considerable distances on them. You would go from the neighbouring village to the next town, to the next city and even travel around the country on them. The cycling horizon stretched endlessly in all directions. Windmills dotted here and there creaked as they turned, whilst I flew along in cycle-track heaven between them. I sensed Rocket Boy ONE was truly in his element in these blissful conditions, as was I. Being blown along by the windmills, I feared we might end up tumbling into one of the canals we were racing along!

Dutch-Japanese friendship
I found the Dutch down-to-earth, open-minded and

generous. I did not have a single bad experience involving the locals during my journey through Holland. They may feel well-disposed towards the Japanese due to the historical relationships that exist between Holland and Japan. Or perhaps there was a profound empathy with a fellow cyclist? Maybe Dutch folk are just like that? It may be one of these factors or it could well be all of them. One rainy day, going into a supermarket to phone the Gerry Ryan Show, the manager came and said he would kindly help me to use the phone. In fact, there was a coffee corner in the supermarket, provided as a service to customers, where you could sit down and relax. The manager told me that this free service was common in the best supermarkets in Holland. They even served me with croissants as a special service. "Meeting a customer who has cycled from Japan is not something that happens every day." Another day, an old man running a petrol station-cum-bike shop readily consented, with a broad smile, to my using a phone there to call the Gerry Ryan Show.

"We've had enthusiastic requests from listeners asking if you could sing a Japanese song, Yas."

I sang 'Koinobori', but in retrospect I realised I had sung the same song at the CNCF banquet in Mongolia. Not that I had any others I could sing on request . . . I sat drinking tea and chatting with the man in the cycle shop and his family for about thirty minutes after the programme finished. They were all so incredibly kind that I felt I was talking to old friends.

My flysheet zip had been getting worse since Sweden and finally started to come adrift in Holland. Unable to mend it, I decided to plead with the campsite manager that night.

"Have you got a safety pin or something else I can use to stop this getting any worse?" The manager, who wore a moustache, told me to bring the flysheet and follow him. Taking it from me he repaired it with his sewing machine in no time at all.

"This ought to keep the rain out until you get to Dublin."

Bridgestone Benelux very kindly looked after me as well.

Henk showed me around every corner of Bridgestone Europe's central warehouse. Nicolette presented me with a red Bridgestone polo shirt. At the sumptuous dinner I enjoyed with these two, I ate local eel. The viscous texture was delicious. My accommodation for the night, the Holiday Inn, was also a present from Bridgestone Benelux. I was unable to meet their boss, Endre, as he was busy, but I must express my profound thanks to him for giving his blessing to all of this.

Clear, cloudy, rain, hail, strong wind, breeze, fine. The sky in Holland changed from hour to hour. It was a bit like being in a washing machine, but the locals just laughed it off, saying, "This is typical Dutch weather."

Bridgestone Belgium

The landscape changed little as I crossed from Holland to Belgium. Belgium looked very much like Holland. I suppose the windmills disappeared, and the cycle tracks were not so well maintained but that was about it. The thing most worthy of mention during my stay in an otherwise unremarkable sojourn in the country was my visit to the Bridgestone Europe Head Office. The Head Office was located there for similar reasons the EU Headquarters and other corporate head offices were in Brussels. I was greeted by Mr Fukuda of Bridgestone. "Well done for coming so far.

You must be absolutely exhausted." For the next two days I was extended all manner of kindness and hospitality. I had long and pleasant chats with Des Collins, the Director (an Irishman to whom I was deeply indebted, as he had been Colm's boss in Ireland. When sponsorship for my project had been approved at European Head Office, it was largely thanks to him that I got it), and other members of staff there. A Japanese member of staff, Nagasawa, took me out to dinner and we had a bucket of the famous mussels steamed in champagne. I stayed that night at the home of the manager of the agricultural tyres department, Stefan. His wife, Katrien, was expecting a baby within the next day or two. The next morning, he took me into town in his car, where I paid my respects to the Manikin Piss. That evening I had dinner in the company of all the Japanese staff at Nagasawa's house, and stayed the night.

Having been so well looked after I had no regrets about missing the Belgian Grand Prix.

I had heard rumours that a senior student friend of mine from university, Kishida, had got a job with an air conditioning company and had been sent to Belgium. I had checked out his contact details through my mum in Japan and it turned out that he was still in Belgium. Kishida's mother was thrilled about it, and had insisted on my visiting him. I had a very tight schedule as it was, but I opened the map and found that Kishida was living in Ostende, smack on the road that led to my final port of call in Eurasia, Calais. It turned out to be an awful day with the bike. The rear wheel spokes bent during the morning (I couldn't repair them on the gear side as I did not have the right tool), the front left carrier suddenly bent and that evening the plastic liner inside the handlebar bag I had just bought in Germany split, a triple whammy. I made it to Kishida's in Ostende after 150 painful kilometres.

"What the heck are you doing in a place like this?"

I burst out laughing. He was still the same old joker. There I was, having met people I had been given introductions to, as well as strangers, right the way across the Eurasian continent, having had all sorts of help and support along the way and slept under scores of different roofs, only to find myself staying, on my last night on the Eurasia continent, in an old friend's house, wearing one of his beautifully white tee-shirts, eating beef and vegetables with Japanese rice and Japanese salted ramen noodles made by his wife who was also expecting a baby two weeks from then.

A mere half-day in France

The young man in a bike shop in Ostende balanced the rear wheel spokes perfectly and free of charge. Rocket Boy ONE was back in top form. A strong north-easterly wind blew along the coast road, catching me and the panniers, square on. It was a perfect day of cycling to end my trans-Eurasian journey on. I turned left off the Ostende coast road, then right after about 5 kilometres. Rolling smoothly along, I suddenly noticed I had arrived in France. Powering westwards, I got directions from a kind man, discovered how well English was spoken, was flustered by the charms of a gorgeous French woman who popped her head out of the passenger window of a Citroen, saw a flock of seagulls take to the air ahead and then away in the distance I saw the funnels of a big ferry. I had arrived in Calais. Suddenly I was on the very edge of the Eurasian continent.

The vast continent I had been pedalling across for 12,000 kilometres melted into the mist as we left the harbour. All that remained was the afterglow of memories glittering like sunlight on the sea.

7

Countdown to Ireland
Nine days to go . . .

The morning sun streamed through the white lace curtains, illuminating the dining room carpet with a dazzling, oval pool of light. Ferries sailed sedately in and out of port beyond the softly fluttering curtains, leaving long wakes as they disappeared from view.

I was intent on trying to cut through my bacon with an inordinately heavy knife and fork. The crispy bacon was just about impossible to cut, and the black pudding jiggled on the plate as I sawed away. This was breakfast at the guesthouse facing the Straits of Dover. I knew that I was in Britain from the solid lump in the pit of my tummy. It was a good guesthouse though. Before leaving Japan my friend, Chris Durbin, had kindly suggested that I stay with his relatives and friends. However, when I phoned from the port the previous evening, he told me, "I'm really sorry, but you can't stay where we arranged because my mate had to go away on urgent business. Would you mind staying at a guesthouse near the port tonight? I'll pay, of course, seeing as I've let you down."

Chris had always been like this. His offers of support were given not because he could afford to be lavish, but simply out of generosity. He was a fine, upstanding English gentleman.

"Don't bother going out tonight. Just eat at a hotel. Enjoy the bright lights of Dover over some delicious wine. I'll pay. Really, it's on me. Look, relax and enjoy yourself. My treat, to say 'well done'."

The Saw Doctors *Green and Red of Mayo*
ALL THE WAY FROM TUAM

Driving was now on the left side of the road and the hills became steep. There were no cycle tracks, and vehicles sped by very close to us. It hadn't been like that for quite some time. Since when, I wondered. Thinking back, it must have been Russia. No, this was just like the roads in Japan. A curious coincidence and something that two islands, separated by the Eurasian continent, shared.

Chris had arranged for me to stay that night with his friend, Paul, in Maidstone, not far from London. Paul's younger sister was a colleague of Chris's. Chris had called Paul a day or two earlier to say I was coming and Paul had agreed to look after me. I was very grateful. He took me to a pub where we drank local Suffolk ale. The beer was pumped up by hand rather than by gas, which made the ale that much smoother. Much like Guinness. For dinner we had English steaks that must have weighed about six hundred grams each but we didn't worry about mad cow disease.

8 days . . .
Morning – The Gerry Ryan Show

"I've just finished eating a British breakfast of bacon and eggs, beans and cereal."

"British breakfast!"

"Eating this sort of breakfast, it seems like I'm almost there in Ireland."

"Last time we talked I seem to remember you had diarrhoea. Did you get rid of that?"

"Yes!"

"How?"

"I went along to a pub in Amsterdam and had a glass of special medicine."

"That'd be Guinness then? Yaz always drinks Guinness when he has any physical ailments."

There were hills and valleys, but no cycle tracks. Seeing as all the roads would be the same, I decided to take the A20, a side road but effectively a shortcut. On a dismal road near London, a woman instructed her kids, "Get him! Take him!" The children proceeded to lob stones at me with all their might. That evening I arrived in London in light rain. As I had been to London many times before it felt strange arriving by bicycle. The air is polluted and many cyclists wear masks like gas masks. It is no laughing matter. Breathing the air really irritated my throat. Waiting casually, as arranged, outside the Angel station, it was not my old friend Chris Durbin who appeared out of the mist but another friend of Warren's, Chris, Chris Ligby.

"Fuckin' great to see you in the saddle here in London."

Chris invited some friends along to the party in the pub he had taken me to for a drink.

It might have had something to do with a sense of relief

from the pressures I had been under, but the Guinness tasted really delicious. And, of course, I was getting closer to the Guinness brewery in Dublin. . . . The next day I visited Mr Keating at the Irish Embassy in London. He was very busy with preparations for the Northern Ireland assembly but kindly took the time to show me around the embassy, including the reading room and reception rooms. The embassy building had once been owned by the Guinness family. I also telephoned Wendy from the CNCF who was then back in Britain. She said that she had been worrying about me since we parted and was relieved to hear my voice. As we talked I was back in Mongolia, with the gentle breeze from the plains clearing my mind.

6 days . . .

I was planning on cycling to Hook Norton, a village the other side of Oxford, to meet up with the Durbin family at Chris's father's house that day. I reckoned it was about 150 kilometres. It was going to be tight, though, as I would have to contend with the morning rush hour in London, as well as the after-effects of last night's Guinness. I got really tired towards the end, but I did make it to the lovely village of Hook Norton, on the edge of the Cotswold hills, that evening. Shortly after being greeted by his smiling dad, Bernard, Chris turned up, hooting the horn of his new Renault, with his wife, Jane, their lovely daughter, Naomi, and the rather more shy Adam. The kids who tumbled out of the car had grown a lot since I had last seen them, but the family was the Durbins I knew well. I felt as if it was only yesterday that we had last seen each other. During the evening Chris and I opened a map to check my route. This took me right back to the time, several years earlier, when we had gone to a map shop in London together. Chris had given me his full support ever since then.

4 days. . .

Yasu, our friend, has the luck of the Irish!

Chris, Jane, B.Durbin, Adam, Naomi (signatures on my helmet)

The Durbin family's cheers and laughter followed as I resumed my journey. I always felt that I wanted to stay with the people I was with. But now, turning right and starting to freewheel downhill, the place and the people I had stayed with vanished, only to be stored as fond memories in my heart. This was always, always the case. I had felt it innumerable times on this trip. Still, there was nothing to be gained by dwelling on the sadness of parting. The only thing to do was to press on.

I cycled on carefully, checking the map at regular intervals. The undulating hills got bigger. The countryside began to remind me a little of Ireland, with sheep in fields surrounded by stone walls. Other cyclists appeared from time to time. The cheese I had for lunch had a sticker on it with the letters GB, which I took to mean Great Britain. Looking at it more closely, however, I saw that in fact it meant 'Great Bike'. Delighted to come across this promotion, I tore it off and stuck it on the back of my helmet. That night I stayed with Auntie D, Jane's auntie. I am sure she had a proper name, but she insisted on being called Auntie D by everyone. Chris had told me 'She's a little eccentric', and indeed she was. She lived in an old cottage outside a village. Inside, the rooms were cluttered. I was not sure how old she was, but although getting on she still had a sharp mind and was physically fit. I learned that she was compiling a history of the village at the time. It seems that she had several adopted children. The son of one of them came over that evening with his family. They were all so bright, kind and cheerful.

3 days . . .

About four miles from Ross-on-Wye in Lea I suddenly remembered the Gerry Ryan Show. I was right next to a garage, so I went in and asked the young girl in the office if I could use the phone.

"No problem," she said, "but it probably stinks of oil."

"I've got some good news." Gerry had added a special section covering my project onto his programme's home page. I was delighted and impressed. There was an outline description of the trip, photographs, reports, an audio section, the itinerary for the journey ahead, as well as a section for messages from the listeners. After cycling a little further I called Colm at Bridgestone. He seemed to have been rushing around making reception arrangements, liaising with the media and organising somewhere for me to stay. I will remain eternally grateful to them as my sponsors. (I appreciate that he had to make considerable efforts to promote Bridgestone on the back of my project.)

Christy Moore *Johnny Conners*

KING PUCK

I crossed from England into Wales where the roads continued to twist, turn, rise and fall. Stone walls increased and more and more sheep dotted the beautiful countryside.

It reminded me so much of Ireland. I would love to return to the area some time. It started raining in earnest as I headed through the valleys of the Black Mountains. In desperation I cycled as far as Brecon, where I bowled into a five-star site supposed to be the 'Best Campsite in Wales'. The flysheet zipper broke and the rain poured in. I couldn't complain. How many times had I opened and closed that zip on the journey?

No doubt it would rain the next day too.

Only 2 days to go . . .

Just before ten thirty the front left-side carrier bent. No, I thought, not again! I wished it would behave itself. Our goal was in sight, after all. We were exhausted, fair enough, but if only it could hang on that little bit longer. You cost me a lot, you know! I pulled straight into a garage in Sennybridge. The father-and-son team there got down to major surgery. Thirty minutes later the operation was over. I insisted on paying them something. They said a few quid would do, and in the end accepted just two pounds. The two kindly allowed me to call the Gerry Ryan Show as well. (From the day before I had seen military vehicles on the road and jet fighters had screamed low overhead. The father told me that there was a big military base nearby.)

The Gerry Ryan Show again. . .

"I've had a succession of problems with my camping gear and bicycle these last few days."

"So, what's happened?"

"My tent flysheet died a death, and the front carrier has been bent since this morning. There is a problem with the front carrier rather than a problem with the Bridgestone bike, just for the record. To fix it, I pulled straight into the garage I'm phoning you from."

"Since you've made it that far, you're going to be all right. The Guinness brewery has made an extra two thousand pints and put them aside for your arrival!"

Then a really serious problem arose. Cycling along in the afternoon I heard a strange noise from the rear carrier. Checking it out at the campsite, I saw that the flange that the rear bracket was fixed to was bent. It was a structural part of the bike itself. I would like to have complained about it, but the flange had been fitted as a customised part after the standard assembly. On top of that the bike had carried a big load for 12,600km. How could I complain? I used a rubber ring as an emergency measure. Since it was part of the bike, the work couldn't really be left to local welders. Now, right at the very end, things were starting to fall apart.

Time to get tough!

The night before I arrived in Ireland I found myself staying on an empty campsite in the rain beset by problems and plunged in emotional turmoil.

Half a day!

I had less than a hundred kilometres to cycle to the port of Fishguard. On the ferry, it would be a matter of hours before I was in Ireland, the land of my dreams. That was all it boiled down to, distance. It would have been nice if matters were that simple. Heaven does not look on us that kindly, however, and things don't always run smoothly. To begin with, it rained all morning. I waited patiently before setting out and when eventually I did, it started bucketing down. Then there was the wind. It was blowing a gale. It came from all four quarters. I felt like a storm-tossed ship. A ship I was trying to power by pedal.

It was a ridiculous idea to leave the A40 and try to take a more direct route into Fishguard, but for some reason I did. The moment I branched off I hit a horrendously steep hill. It proved too difficult. There was no way I could physically cope with a hill like that first thing in the morning. There wasn't a single signpost. I pushed on as far as I could, and just when it seemed I was completely lost, I hit the A40 again. Which just goes to prove the saying 'more haste less speed'. If the road I had taken had been the shortest and the most direct, then the main road would naturally have followed it. The town would lie along the main road anyway. "Use your head, you clown!" I chastised myself. The main road from there on was, as expected, quite smooth. The rain lashing down stung, but the countryside was as green as ever and looked so lush.

I waited for a telephone callback from the Gerry Ryan Show at a Ford dealer near Haverford West, but there was no news at all. I might have been a bit late calling. Staff at the dealership told me there were ferry cancellations that morning due to the stormy weather. Concerned at my apparent plight, the young girl on reception called the ferry company for me and confirmed that the afternoon ferry would sail. Thanks to everyone at Ford in Haverford West!

It didn't take long from there. The rain stopped and my mood brightened as we flew towards Fishguard down a gentle hill. The town attracted us like a powerful magnet.

The last hill downward stretched for about 10 kilometres. Then suddenly we were at the harbour.

I wept in spite of myself when I saw the Irish tricolour on the ferry.

I could almost reach out and touch Ireland.

8

Ireland!

On a raging sea

The ferry raised anchor and swept out into the bay shuddering deeply as it turned and headed west. I stood alone on the deck, my thoughts flying from the cliffs away to the east to the sea to the west. If the bay were someone's mouth, then the ferry was a plum stone Fishguard spat into the huge swells of the stormy sea. The misery of the morning followed me out to sea. The sides of the boat shook violently in the dense fog, obliterating memories, thoughts of Inishmore, and sentimentality. I fled inside.

Sitting on a sofa in the lounge, I saw screaming passengers come rushing inside. One flushed, bald old man who looked the worse for wear, possibly after a rough night, noisily deposited what looked like the balance of whatever ale he had left in his stomach across the floor. I heard it. Then I smelt it. In danger of succumbing to the nausea I quietly lay down on the sofa, shut my eyes and willed sweeter memories to come to mind.

Wandering around in the darkness behind my eyelids I

visualised the vibrations shaking me to the pit of my stomach. Travelling through my groin the vibrations made their way down my thighs, fizzing the lactic acid in every muscle cell. At an even deeper level I anticipated those tired, taut yet confident, pedal power cells waiting to welcome me. I was dragged back to the surface, however, by noises demanding my attention.

In my mind's eye I saw a thousand marbles, rattled by the waves. Inside each sparkling, jade marble, glowed a sweet memory . . .There was Ono, laughing as he held a pair of Japanese builders' shoes he kept as a souvenir, Watatsune's warnings about diarrhoea, Jana's homemade scones, the thunder of truck horns, the Great Wall in the rain, the puncture-repair maestro, the sautéed beef with pepper in black bean sauce, the rosy faces, the *sheh shehs,* my first night in the tent, Byalma's worried face, Gobi Desert sand, the colour of the wind in Mongolia, the rutted tracks, the sunny faces in the gers, the bleating of sheep, the smell of sheep, the fresh well water, the confrontation in Sainshand, Batsaihan's white teeth, Bahtimpkh and Tsagan rolling around in the tent, the camels, the moonlight, Kyokushuzan, everyone at CNCF, the starry sky over Ulan Bator, Ganbator, the four young boys who pushed me up a hill, radiant green Sübaatar Station, the tanks in Kyakhta, Russian biscuits, *shashlik,* the hail in Ulan Ude, Tora and Albina, my vodka baptism, the blueness and depth of Lake Baikal, *omul,* Baikal water, the Baikalsk Municipal Offices, the Baikal hills, Irkutsk and the Angara, the old 'scales' man, hot-blooded Victor, the warm welcome in Kansk, the party at a bus stop, Andrei the policeman, the kindness of Marietta, the Kemerovo incident, the maggot conductor, revisiting Krasnoyarsk, Olga and Volodya, Elena and the Guinness, giant mosquitoes, *priama, priama*, silver birches, *davai, davai*, Mr Johnson, mud-bespattered, desperate pedalling, crossing Kazakhstan, *morozhenoe*, Ladas, Ladas, Russian power stations, *spasiva, spasiva*, calling the Gerry Ryan Show from Celyabinsk, voices from Japan, Ural flowers, the Pedalling Dutchmen, recurring problems with the bike, the evening sun over the Volga, the Kolya family's fresh eggs, being besieged by vodka, *Na zdorove!* (did everyone really like vodka that much?), the shower in the car wash, sushi in Moscow, Ireland in Moscow, the night of Guinness, on the road repairs, twang!, opulent St Petersburg, *Do svidaniya, Russia!*, Helsinki salmon, Bridgestone, the delicious food prepared by Tapani, the fishermen in Stockholm, Maria cycling up hills, the mirror-like lake surface, nostalgia in Copenhagen, German wine, being chased off the autobahn, Dutch cheese, Dutch cycle tracks, Bridgestone Head Office, Kishida, Calais, Dover, bacon, steak, Chris in London, Chris's family in Hook Norton, D, rain, wind, tyre friction noises, saddle vibration, lunches, breakfasts, the tent, and the wind, the wind, the wind . . .

How long had I been gazing at the marbles? The moment the marble with memories of Fishguard appeared, all the other marbles suddenly ceased rattling around as if they had been waiting for that moment and simply vanished like soap bubbles. The boat had made it across the stormy sea. The lateral shaking had subsided and it seemed we were close to land.

Running up onto the deck, there before my eyes lay the green countryside of Ireland. The scene was flooded with golden evening sunlight. A big flock of seagulls flew around overhead, screaming a welcome across the sparkling golden sea. Words cannot express what I felt at that moment.

I had made it to Ireland. Yes, yes, yes!
I'd done it. I'd really done it.

Landing
(There didn't seem to be anyone waiting for me!)

It wasn't asking too much to expect someone to turn up, was it? Perhaps it would be Colm from Bridgestone or a member of staff from the Gerry Ryan Show? They had promised they would. Confident that someone would be there, I emerged from the car deck and stood on Irish ground at last. Looking around there wasn't a soul to be seen. I thought that they might be out of sight behind one of the nearby containers so I went and had a look. There was no one there either. What had happened? Having pedalled so far, I was quite naturally saddened at the prospect. I felt wretched but at least both feet were on Irish soil. That was the single most important thing, I decided, as I stamped down on the ground repeatedly with both feet. It might have been asphalt, but I kicked and kicked, my head in the clouds. I'm sure this strange spectacle caught people's attention. Anyway, a Mazda drove up, the door opened, and a middle-aged man and a slim, pretty woman got out. It was Willy and Ciara.

"Hey, Yaz. Good to meet you. I'm Willy, the producer of the Gerry Ryan Show. We were waiting to welcome you in the arrivals lounge. They've got a live video of one of your favourites, Christy, up on the big screen to welcome you. We waited for ages. We were getting worried so we came over. Now here you are, waiting all alone." So the reception might have been as I had dreamt it would be; I could have taken my bike into the arrivals lobby where the songs and guitar

223

chords of Christy would have been playing. Others would have been waiting there too, greeting me with smiling faces. That would have been such a lovely arrival! "Anyway, let's go to the hotel. Follow the car." Ciara's face shone in the sunshine from the west. I followed them for about a kilometre to the Great Southern Hotel, situated on a cliff top. The staff were waiting to welcome me with champagne. "It's been an incredibly long journey. Well done. Fantastic! We're honoured to have you staying with us at the hotel."

I was inundated with delicious champagne and posed for endless photographs. I even got to sign and write a message in the guest book. My status had indeed gone up a peg or two! Colm from Bridgestone arrived a bit later than he had planned. This was the first time I had actually seen him. He looked younger than I had imagined. It was thanks to him that the trip had become such a significant project. I couldn't even begin to express how grateful I was to Colm. The first thing he blurted out to me was 'Unbelievable!!!'

Guinness for strength

That refreshing feeling . . . the way the head sinks slowly, steadily, like a gold stage curtain. The creamy bubbles stick to the tip of your nose, then drip off, like whipped cream. And then there is the slight bitterness imparted by the chocolaty taste.

I had drunk Guinness in a number of places. Osaka, Tokyo, Beijing, Novosibirsk, Moscow, St Petersburg, Copenhagen, Amsterdam and London. The closer I got to Dublin, the noticeably better the taste had become but those pints could not hold a candle to the real stuff. You can only drink this Guinness in Ireland. Aaaaahh, there's nothing like it. This was what I came for . . . Guinness for strength, for spiritual fortification to carry on pedalling. It was acting as a stabiliser to support pedalling in my heart. I felt completely restored to health. I had dinner with Willy, Ciara and Colm and we discussed, among other things, arrangements for the following day. The feta cheese, salmon and other delicacies served by the hotel were all complimentary. We had coffee afterwards in the hotel bar. I, naturally, had Irish coffee. The band in the function room stopped and Willy was introduced. Using a microphone, he proceeded to tell the story of my journey to the other guests who happened to be there and then he introduced me. Getting up onto the stage, it seemed that I was talking to a party of veterans, a Golden Age tour. Rows of wrinkly faces peered up at me. A presentation from the hotel was followed by some short speeches. Everyone clapped and cheered. The Guinness might have had something to do with my feeling of being in a dream. Leaving the stage, I was surrounded by old ladies wanting to shake my hand.

"I'm a listener to the Gerry Ryan Show, you know. I've been concerned about you since the moment you set out. Now you're here, standing right here and looking great. I'm so pleased."

The old lady had a tear in her eye as she gripped my hand. Her feelings were very important to me, but the dance with her in the party that followed was unforgettable for other reasons.

A number of other people came rushing to the hotel just to meet and congratulate me. They said that they had been following my journey very closely. This pleased me. The Guinness they bought for me was the most delicious. Willy and Ciara left, leaving Colm and me drinking Irish whiskey and chatting for ages. One of Colm's stories stayed with me, in spite of my drunken state.

"Why did we decide to sponsor you? Really because Bridgestone is laying out huge sums of money sponsoring Formula 1 but the people seeing those races are mainly in the 18 to 35 age bracket and they are mostly men. The Gerry Ryan Show listeners, on the other hand, include everyone from kids to adults, male and female. So, as most people drive cars, they will all have to choose tyres at some time or other. I am wiser than most staff members who are putting money into F1."

Passing through the smiling arch

I now had to travel from Rosslare on the south-east coast of Ireland to Greystones, south of Dublin. According to the map it was about 150 kilometres. Seeing as I had only just arrived in Ireland I wanted to do slightly less pedalling but I simply couldn't change this part of the itinerary.

It was Thursday so I had to arrive in Dublin the next day. There is no Gerry Ryan show on a Saturday. The more ground I covered that day, the less I would have to cover the next day and this would help ensure that I arrived in Dublin some time the following morning. The arrangements were quite delicate. My mother, my aunt Mitsuyo, Keiko (now married to my younger brother), Maria, Maria's parents, her younger sister and her boyfriend, as well as other assorted friends were arriving in Dublin. It all meant that I had little or no flexibility. In fact, this route was completely different to the one I originally intended to take. I had initially planned to take the Holyhead ferry directly to Dublin, but having cycled this far, both the Gerry Ryan Show and Bridgestone suggested I travel through Ireland so that my arrival could be celebrated by the Irish.

As Gerry had said on his show there would be 'Irish smiles on the streets' waiting to welcome me. Seeing these faces would be more than enough for me.

Pedal on

I was live on the Gerry Ryan Show from the lobby of the hotel after breakfast.

"Welcome to Ireland! You're here at last, Yaz! How are you?"

"I had my first glass of Irish Guinness last night. It was fuckin' lovely!"

"I want anyone living along Yaz's route today, or anyone driving past him, to cheer him on."

The old folk from the bar last night were interviewed too. After we had finished taping the programme there were endless pictures with the guests at the hotel. I was temporarily blinded by the flashes from the camera. I set off to cries of encouragement from the assembled crowd. Colm's Ford led for the first 10km, hazard lights flashing.

No doubt in response to Gerry's appeal on the radio, car after car honked its horn. Drivers and people lining the road shouted, "Well done Yaz!!!" as we passed. It went on and on. I passed through a tunnel of smiling faces, encouragement and admiration. I did high fives with drivers and people standing and clapping beside the road. I smiled at all the camera lenses. Feelings spilt over in a tear or two as I pedalled by.

Pedal on, pedal on, pedal on . . .

Willy and Ciara found me again just before midday (being

a bit of an emotional wreck I had managed to lose my way).
I was on the Gerry Ryan Show live by a roadside in the teeth
of a gale.

"You didn't get lost in the Gobi Desert, but get to Ireland
and you do! What happened?"

"I blame last night's Guinness."

I met up again with Willy and Ciara near the town of
Enniscorthy. A woman (a listener to the programme) in a
BMW standing next to them was waiting to have lunch with
me. Sitting in the pub chatting over a chicken curry pie, her
son, who was at primary school, came over.

"He was totally set on meeting you," said his mum,
presenting me with a litre bottle of 7UP.

There were still another 90 kilometres from here to
Greystones. I felt confident, however, knowing my goal was
within range and that there would be plenty of support from
everyone.

Pedal on, pedal on, pedal on . . .

The wind was overwhelming and the rain fell in sheets.
This was Ireland all right. It was as cold as it had ever been
on the trip. There were fewer car horns than I had heard
during the morning, but many cars still beeped as they
passed by. They helped revitalise me. Urged on entirely by
the support I was getting, I didn't really take in the scenery
around me. The important scenery was the smiling faces of
the supporters themselves. I had imagined scenes like this in
my dreams during the journey.

Towards evening pedal power flagged so I took
impromptu breaks stopping to chat to the people standing
and clapping on the roadside. A young man in a red Primera
who was working in Wexford, said, "I worried most about

you in the Gobi Desert. I'm glad you made it safely. Well done, Yaz!"

Another young guy, waiting for me leaning against a small truck, handed me a piece of paper with 'GO ON, THE YAZ!!!' written on it.

The other side of the Wicklow Hills there was a couple waiting for me in a Polo.

"We stayed in a different hotel in Rosslare last night. We rushed over this morning when we heard about you on the Gerry Ryan Show, but you'd left. Siberia sounded really hard. We were worried about what might happen to you."

Cycling down a gentle hill about 15 kilometres from Greystones, a young cyclist wearing jazzy cycling gear came up alongside me and called out, '"Yaz! I've been waiting two years for you to come this way!" It seems that the Gerry Ryan Show had been on every morning where Richard worked, and they had to listen to it, even when they didn't want to. As a fellow cyclist, he had taken a keen interest in me from the first time I had appeared on the Gerry Ryan Show. He knew I was passing that day and that I was heading for Greystones that night, so had taken time off work. Greystones was a long way from where he lived, which meant a long round trip, but he didn't care about the distance. He wanted to guide me to my destination hotel. He was a great guy. I had dinner at the hotel after a leisurely shower. (My accommodation had been arranged by the Gerry Ryan Show.) After dinner I went to the pub where I met yet another listener, Paul. He had listened avidly to news of my progress. He was so excited about the whole thing he treated me to seven pints of Guinness. Drinking so much, I had doubts I would cope with the final leg the following day.

"Well done, Yaz!!" Shouts were still echoing in the hotel yard as I went up to my room, head spinning.

So, it was turning out brilliantly. Ireland was, as I knew it to be, great. I had come to the conclusion, in Russia, that the world isn't that bad. Whilst I concluded this in Russia, it was in Ireland, among the Irish, that I realised what it really meant. It made the whole journey worthwhile.

Straight to RTE

Whenever I had gone to sleep, be it in Mongolia, Baikal or in the middle of Siberia, I had told myself what time I wanted to get up and without fail I had woken up at the right time. The morning sun, birdsong and fear of being assaulted had probably prompted me to get up. How I woke up at the right time after cycling, drinking and talking as much as I had the previous day remains a mystery. The soft morning sunlight was streaming in through the windows, of course, but I couldn't help feeling it was more likely the spirits of the seven pints I had consumed the previous night.

It was the day of the final leg. Cycle safely, I reminded myself, as I launched out. Go for it!

Pedal on, pedal on, pedal on . . .

Greystones aglow in the morning light was still asleep. Leaving town, I found myself faced with a very steep hill. Hills like this, though, were nothing to me. Had I not struggled up and over hill after hill after hill? And today was, after all, the final day. I reached Bray at about eight o'clock and the road was packed with commuters and students. The road was a torrent of angry horns. No one took the slightest notice of me. Come to think about it, my journey had begun with honking horns in China. They would still be honking.

The honking and passing cheers of encouragement began shortly after I left Bray. Everyone seemed to be up. Or the Gerry Ryan Show had started. The morning sun cut through the trees, striping the road with a zebra pattern. I would have to make a left turn somewhere soon. It was already getting on for nine o'clock, though, the pre-arranged time. Best to check with someone so as not to mess things up at a time like this. I spotted a lady standing right on the corner ahead. "Hey, it's Yaz! Well done. You made it. Gerry Ryan just said on the radio that if anyone saw you we had to help and give you directions. Seems you're a bit late aren't you?"

(Yes. I am late. I really don't have time to stop and chat to you right now)

"But anyway, you must have so many stories about your journey. How about coming and having a cup of tea with me?"

Pedal on, pedal on, pedal on . . .

I turned left there taking the road west. The road looked vaguely familiar. Hadn't I been along it after visiting RTE for the first time? Yes, that was it. I just had to turn right off this section of dual carriageway and go down a gentle hill. I suddenly spotted a TV mast. Yup, this was it.

The receptionist at the radio station, the one who had helped by copying my travel plans for me was smiling as I came in. "Well done, Yaz."

Thanks Gerry
Making my way along to the Gerry Ryan Show office I came across a tall man wearing a Garda uniform, and a short Asian gentleman. The Asian man turned out to be Yoichi Hoashi, Japanese owner of a Japanese restaurant Gerry frequented.

231

He was co-starring on the programme along with his celebration sushi and saké. Michael was a Dublin motorcycle policeman. Colm, through a contact, had specially arranged for a motorbike escort to accompany me to the Guinness hop store!!!

I went down the stairs to the studio. Passing several soundproofed studios I came to an open door. Going through it I saw Gerry waving to me from the other side of a soundproof glass screen. He was, as he had promised, broadcasting me live. How often had we dreamed of that day? "Hey, Yaz! After cycling thousands of kilometres, we meet at last. What about this for a sumptuous breakfast!?" said Gerry. We opened the saké. Ciara, sitting next to me, said, "It says One Cup Ozeki on the bottle. Ozeki's your name isn't it?" *Kanpai,* and *Slainte!* "Gerry, Yaz has got something he has brought as a present for you all the way from Japan. Let's open it live on air." Gerry looked puzzled as he removed the underwear from the wrapping. "Some present. But I'm mystified, Yaz. Explain."

"They're evidence of my having cycled here from Japan. Smelly, living proof."

"Hang on there a moment. You're saying you've worn this old underwear from Japan?"

"The proof."

"Well, thanks for the unique present."

We enjoyed the sushi party.

"The Garda has come along especially for Yaz today, but not because he has done anything wrong. The rider will escort Yaz to the Guinness hop store. The most delicious Guinness in the world is waiting for Yaz at the factory." Turning away to leave the studio, I heard Gerry over the speakers, saying, "I'd like to commemorate Yaz's long and wonderful adventure by playing one of his favourite tunes for you all." It was Christy Moore's 'The Voyage'.

Michael quietly started the motor on his bike and led the way. The blue light rotated silently on the back of the bike. Ahead of me the police bike, behind me the RTE radio car. Paul Russell leaned out of the rear window taking photos of me. Without him this would never have got off the ground.

The road was busy, but I felt quite safe. *I had goose bumps.* A young man in a lorry in the oncoming lane was shouting to me, white teeth gleaming. *I felt hot tears welling up uncontrollably.*

Coming up to junctions, Michael would accelerate, switch on his wailing siren and position himself on the crossing. Standing in the middle of the road he stopped all the traffic with his right hand.

Once we had crossed the junction, he would overtake us swiftly and silently resuming his position in front. This was quite stressful, in fact, because I couldn't pause for a rest!

To my relief, though, we had almost reached our goal. No need to worry any more about what I had to buy for dinner or about looking for a campsite. I would get there, and that would be it.

The tears kept coming. The wind was on our side, pushing us ever onwards.

The traffic built up as we got into the city centre, along with the horns, flashing headlights and shouts of encouragement. "Well done, Yaz!". The smiling faces and waving arms went on and on.

I was too ecstatic to acknowledge them and I was getting really worked up as I pedalled along. Now and then my mind simply went blank. Into this vacuum burst memories of places I had been such as Siberia and mornings in Mongolia. *My fingertips shook with the emotion.* On Patrick Street we headed towards the Liffey. The old man I had met at the restaurant in Tientsin was reaching out to me with chapped hands, wishing me well. *My heart was soaring.*

Pedal on, pedal on, pedal on.

A child holding her mum's hand was waving vigorously and smiling at me. I took a left turn into High Street. One old woman was shouting at the top of her voice for some reason. A Mongolian boy, laughing as he rode alongside me, was wishing me well. *"Sain, Sain."*

Pedal on, pedal on, pedal on.

The road curved gently into West Thomas Street. The Russian women standing next to the bus stop were shouting *"Davai, Davai!"* to me. The emptiness inside my head spread to the rest of my body. I could no longer focus on anything. I could see nothing. Absolutely nothing. The next moment I was immersed in creamy bubbles of Guinness. I saw myself standing there beyond the creamy head, proudly holding a pint of Guinness up to the sky. A flash of lightning illuminated the gloom around me. Rocket Boy One seemed relieved too. Well done, old boy. This is the final braking.

There was Maria, eyes full of tears, and Keiko, standing next to her. This was such a great show. Gene was there also and CNCF staff. The attaché to the Japanese embassy turned up. There were loads of reporters and Colm, keeping Bridgestone in the limelight. Suddenly Ciara was in front of me holding the microphone. They were there to record the event for the final programme. And wasn't that Kevin speaking to Katarina? Everyone was drinking Guinness.

Everyone was smiling. The chink of pint glasses meeting could be heard all round the place. And I was still immersed in creamy bubbles of Guinness. One hand tapped me lightly on the shoulder. Looking back I saw Odysseus, having come to the end of his travels, beaming at me with joy.

Epilogue

Return to Joyce Tower

Yes, in terms of distance I had covered 12,935.2km, but how many kilometres had I covered on my journey of the heart? My starting point had been the idea that I wanted to 'kick down' the distance by cycling it myself, to discover what lay in the great gap that existed between Japan and myself and Ireland. The gap, that distance, seemed to be nothing more than the distance between what I longed for, Ireland, and what I found so frustrating, Japan. Perhaps this was something I had known all along or theoretically at least. In the event what did I discover pedalling between the two countries?

I came to the conclusion that the more I pedal, the more I get to know that the world isn't that bad. The more I pedal, the clearer this becomes. The world may not be perfect, but it's certainly not a complete mess. People in every part of the world have their own culture and way of life. One is no better than the other. Variety is the important thing. Though our cultures, our styles may vary, humanity and that which lies at the centre of all our worlds is essentially the same. Whichever country I travelled to, the people and the world they live in, were characterised by the natural kindness we all have. What carried my bicycle forwards was this kindness. I simply sat on the saddle. It was the borderless kindness and the smiling faces that rolled the snowman of my dreams along, helping it grow. These thoughts crystallised in my mind in the middle of Siberia and I began to see Japan and Ireland in this light. Japan is an amazing country in so many ways. China, Mongolia and Russia are equally amazing, of course. In so far as the world isn't such a bad place, I believe I could get along with people anywhere. The question, ultimately, is which way of life suits me best? For my part, this is not in Japan, Russia, Holland, Denmark, or England. It is life in Ireland. This is a purely personal preference, nothing more, nothing less. You can only make judgements about countries using your own criteria, but for me that question is now irrelevant. As the country I was born in, the place I came from, I inevitably expected a great deal from Japan. Perhaps this was why I had seen Japan in such a negative light. On my cycling trip, I made an effort to view all countries dispassionately. It was Ireland and those smiling faces that marked the end of my journey and that confirmed my ideas. It really all comes down to the questions who and what am I. It is enough that I live my life to the fullest as a human being and as a Japanese person. I will simply strive to achieve that. It may be a highly subjective, and overly simple conclusion, but in reality that it is all there is. The greatest reward I earned from this journey was not to know it theoretically, but to actually feel what that means. I learned from the trip that Japan and Ireland are simply what they are, whatever I may say on the subject. The distance between them remains the same. One thing I know is that I grew much closer to Ireland, my goal and to Japan, the country I came from. I don't know when it happened, but the door I passed through when I left Japan was opened and sunlight from the East gradually started streaming through. The more distant Japan was, the closer it felt. Ireland, which lay ahead, lit the path before me with a different radiance, another hue. Now I had arrived I saw new doors opening. Now I had to continue to grow and discover a new 'me'. Always embracing the never-ending dream. Wherever I go there will be nowhere bigger than the Eurasian continent. For a while at least, things had come full circle. However the wheels at my destination had already started turning, taking me even further from my starting point. My feet were at last planted on solid ground. Yes.

* * *

Congratulations from listeners

I will end this story with the following quotes from letters of congratulations received from listeners to the Gerry Ryan Show, as well as messages written on my helmet by everyone who was there for me when I arrived.

Welcome to Ireland – it seems a long way to travel for a Guinness, but hey, I am sure it was worth it. Well done.

Shelly

Bualadh bós. Well done Yaz, fair play to ya, boy!

Mary

Well done, Yaz, you made it. Hope you enjoy Ireland, and I don't think you're mad . . .

Deirdre (Sligo)

Congratulations on the journey. Your weekly messages have given hope to all us 9 – 5 workers trapped on 'the escalator'.

Paul

Ore wa Nihon de go-nen gurai sunde-ita, shikashi kimi no you na yatsu wa atta-koto nai! Honto-ni taishita-mon daze!!!

   Nihon ni ita toki, yoku jitensha ryoko shita. Ikkai Tokyo kara Shizuoka made.

   Cork ni sunde-iru. Zehi oide kudasai!! Tanoshimi-shite-masu. (I lived in Japan for about five years, but I never met anyone quite like you! What you've done is brilliant!!! I rode a bike in Japan. I once cycled from Tokyo to Shizuoka. I live in Cork. Make sure you come and see me. Look forward to seeing you.)

John Thompson, Cork

My wife and I first heard of your exploits listening to Gerry Ryan on 2FM whilst touring in Ireland in May this year.

   We have since returned to Australia and have continued to follow your journey on the Internet.

   What a great effort and you don't seem to have lost your sense of humour at all – there must be a little bit of Irish in you.

Robin and Maureen Fitzgerald,
Victoria, Australia

Fitz in New York wants to know 'Is your arse sore?'

Yasuyuki Ozeki

Messages on my helmet

Yaz

Here at last with Guinness and *Céad Míle Fáilte*

> *John + Karen*
> *(Managing Director of Bridgestone/Firestone Ireland)*

You fell off the escalator onto your bike; now you must get into the lift. Have a wonderful life.

> *Colm, Anne-Marie + Dean*
> *(Bridgestone/Firestone Ireland)*

Fuck everything except Yaz!

> *Gerry Ryan*

Congrats from CNCF Dublin,

> *Maria*

I never thought you'd do it, but I'm very glad you did. Congratulations from

> *Alva MacSherry*
> *(The Irish Times)*

The greatest destination is the journey home. Welcome to your spiritual home, Ireland

> *Liam Campbell*
> *(Bord Failte – Irish Tourist Board)*

All's well that ends well!

> *Frank X. O'Donoghue*
> *(Department of Foreign Affairs)*

Appendix

EQUIPMENT LIST

A • BICYCLE AND BICYCLE TOOLS

1   Acoustic Motor Bike (Mountain Bike)
    Bridgestone Tailor Made, Rocket Boy ONE

2   Bicycle Helmet
    Second-hand from Harding's Bikes, Dublin,
    painted with Eurasian Continent by
    Mr. Warren Popelier

3   Bicycle Bags (Front and Rear)
    ORTLIEB Bike Packer/Front Roller

4   Front/Rear Bag Racks
    MINOURA Steel Front/Rear Bag Racks

5   Handle Bar Bag and its Carrier
    MONT-BELL Touring Front Bag and its Carrier

6   Speed and Distance Meter
    CATEYE CC-AT100 (Cycle Computer)

7 Spare Tyres and Inner Tubes
   IRC Block and Slick Tyres x 8,
   Bridgestone Tubes x 4

8 Other Spare Parts and Tools
   Spare Spokes and Spoke Key, Screw and
   Screwdriver, Bolt, Adjustable Spanner
   Allen Keys, Chain Links, Puncture Repair Kit,
   Handy Air Pump x 2, Oil, Grease,
   Spare Brake Pad, Wires

9 Cable Lock

10 Pathfinder Altimeter Watch
   CASIO Pro-Trek

11 Compass
   SUUNTO

12 Cycle Bag
   Ostrich

B • SLEEPING ARRANGEMENTS

1 Tent
   L.L. Bean Free Standing Ultralight Tent

2 Mattresses
Therm-a-Rest Ultralite Long with
repair kit

3 Sleeping-Bags
 MONT-BELL U.L. Down Hugger,
 MONT-BELL Gore-Tex Side Zip Sleeping
 Bag Cover

4 MINI MAGLITE

C • COOKING UTENSILS

1 Stoves
 COLEMAN PEAK 1(ApexII Triple-Fuel Stove),
 TRANGIA No.27-2

2 Fuel Bottle
 SIGG

3 Water Bottles and Holders

4 Light Weight Collapsible Water Container

5 Field Knife
 GERBER

6 Swiss Knife Victrinox Camper

7 Other Cooking Utensils
 Aluminium Spoon and Fork, Plastic Mug

8 Salt and Pepper, Cooking Oil etc

9 Water Filter Katadyn Mini Filter

D • FIRST AID, WASHING, VARIOUS

1 Medical Kit
>Band-Aids, Bandage, Adhesive Tape,
>Poison Remover

2 Medicine
>Diarrhoea Tablets, Flu Pills, Insect Repellent,
>Antibiotic Pills

3 Emergency Food

4 Insect Head Set

5 Washbag with Toothbrush, Toothpaste,
Soap, etc

6 Toilet Paper

7 Mini Nail Clippers

8 Safety Pins, Needles, Thread

9 Ear-Plugs

10 Super Quick Adhesive

11 Maps

12 Notebooks for Memorandum
and Diary

13 Book
> The Odyssey, Homer

14 Other
> Passport, Credit Card, Cash,
> International Driving License,
> Card clearly stating Blood Group,
> Travel Insurance Card,
> Favourite Music List

E • CAMERA AND FILMS

1 Camera
> RICOH GR1

2 Films Positive x 28, Negative x 1

F • CYCLING CLOTHES

1 T-Shirts x 3, Short Pants x 2
> MONT-BELL

2 Long Pants and Shirts for city walking

3 Sports Training Wear
> UMBRO

4 Fleece Pullover
> MONT-BELL

5 Inner Shirts and Pants
MONT-BELL

6 GORE-TEX Rain Jacket and Pants
MONT-BELL

7 Cycling Gloves
Perl Izumi, OGK

8 Socks
MONT-BELL

9 Underwear

10 Shoes
L.L. Bean Mountain Treads, Teva Sandals

11 Sunglasses and spare glasses

WEATHER AND DISTANCE CHARTS

Date	Location	Day Distance (km)
Apr.16	**Osaka - Kobe**	**42.8**
Apr.18	Tangu - Tianjin	61.2
Apr.19	Tianjin - Beijing	144.2
Apr.20	Beijing	18.7
Apr.22	Beijing - Great Wall	80.0
Apr.23	Great Wall - Huai'an	106.1
Apr.24	Huai'an - Xuanhua	113.2
Apr.25	Xuanhua - Oahar	67.0
Apr.26	Oahar - Jining	87.8
Apr.28	Jining - ?	123.4
Apr.29	? - On the grass	126.4
Apr.30	On the grass - Erenhot	192.6
May.1	Erenhot	1.0
May.2	Zamn-Ude - No Where	95.6
May.3	No Where - Orgon	83.4
May.4	Orgon - Sainshand	63.5
May.5	Sainshand - A Ger	117.8
May.7	A Ger - A Lake	89.8
May.8	A Lake - Another Ger	106.0
May.9	Another Ger - Xangai	123.8
May.10	Xangai - Ulaan Baatar	80.2
May.17	Ulaan Baatar - Where?	140.6
May.18	Where? - Darkhan	101.6
May.19	Darkhan - Suchbaatar	107.8
May.20	Nausiki - Kyakhta	41.9
May.21	Kyakhta - Gusinoozersk	130.7
May.22	Gusinoozersk - Ulan Ude	117.0
May.23	Ulan Ude - Selengisk	70.0
May.25	Selengisk - Baikal 1	98.0
May.26	Baikal 1 - Baikal Special	104.8
May.28	Baikal Special - Kuptuk	125.7
May.29	Kuptuk - Irkutsk	112.1
June.1	Irkutsk - Mihanpovka	136.1
June.2	Mihanpovka - A valley	125.1
June.3	A valley - Tulun	186.1
June.4	Tulun - Zamzor	182.7
June.5	Zamzor - Taishet	97.3
June.6	Taishet - Kansk	169.2
June.7	Kansk - Uyar	140.0
June.8	Uyar - Krasnoyarsk	122.5
June.10	Krasnoyarsk - Achinsk	188.2

Total Distance (km	Weather
42.8	**Super Fine**
104.2	Very Fine
248.2	OK
266.9	Fine
346.9	Rain/Thunder
453.0	Rain/Wind
566.2	Fine
633.2	Fine & dry
721.0	Lovely!
844.4	Rain
970.8	Windy
1,163.4	From Fine to Shit
1,164.4	Very Fine
1,260.0	Super Fine and Super Dry
1,343.4	Extremely Dry
1,406.9	Strong Wind
1,524.7	Well, all right
1,614.5	Hot!
1,720.5	Dry & Fine
1,844.3	Fresh!
1,924.5	Windy
2,080.8	Very good!
2,182.4	Strong Wind
2,290.2	Fine, Fine, Fine
2,332.1	Cloudy
2,462.8	Snow to Sun
2,579.8	Snow & Cloud
2,649.8	Fuckin' rain
2,747.8	Cloudy
2,852.6	OK
2,978.3	Very Fine
3,090.4	Fine to Hot
3,226.5	Warm
3,351.6	OK
3,537.7	Cloudy to Fine
3,720.4	Strong Rain to Very Fine
3,817.7	Cold
3,986.9	Slightly rain
4,126.9	Fuckin' rain
4,249.4	Very Fine
4,437.6	Sun and Slightly Rain

Date	Location	Day Distance (km)
June.11	Achinsk - Itatskij	107.0
June.12	Itatskij - Usmanka	142.2
June.13	Usmanka - Kemerovo	150.3
June.16	(Krasnoyarsk)Taiga - Jurga	90.3
June.17	Jurga - Novosibirsk	184.8
June.19	Novosibirsk	4.1
June.20	Novosibirsk - Kabinetnoe	141.2
June.21	Kabinetnoe - Ubinskoje	131.1
June.22	Ubinskoje - Nowhere	156.0
June.23	Nowhere - Ust-Tarka	158.0
June.24	Ust-Tarka - Omsk	191.7
June.26	Omsk - Before Kazafstan	131.0
June.27	Before Kazafstan - Znamenskoje	139.4
June.28	Znamenskoje - Back to Russia	145.0
June.29	Back to Russia - Vargasi	146.5
June.30	Vargasi - Miskino	155.3
July.1	Miskino - Celjabinsk	162.6
July.4	Celjabinsk - Ural	125.4
July.5	Ural - Ural	145.0
July.6	Ural - Ufa	164.6
July.7	Ufa - Asjanovo	146.1
July.8	Asjanovo - ?	131.8
July.9	? - In a Valley	141.7
July.10	In a Valley - Kazan	149.6
July.12	Kazan - Nowhere	137.5
July.13	Nowhere - Close to Volga	151.1
July.14	Close to Volga - Niznij Novgorod	119.3
July.15	Niznij Novgorod - Simoncevo	159.3
July.16	Simoncevo - Petushky	158.2
July.17	Petushky - Moskva	136.0
July.21	Moskva - Close to Volga	151.9
July.22	Close to Volga - Vydropuzhsk	133.1
July.23	Vydropuzhsk - Cows	152.7
July.24	Cows - Spasskaya Polist	155.9
July.25	Spasskaya Polist - St.Peterburg	159.3
July.29	St.Peterburg - Vyborg	136.0
July.30	Vyborg - Kotka	137.1
July.31	Kotla - Helsinki	130.3
Aug-02	Stockholm	30.2
Aug-04	Stockholm	005.2
Aug-05	Stockholm - Sibble	56.3
Aug-06	Sibble - Horn	80.3

Total Distance (km	Weather
4,544.6	Rain
4,686.8	Strong Rain to OK
4,837.1	Lovely!
4,927.4	Brilliant!
5,112.2	Very Fine
5,116.3	Fine
5,257.5	OK
5,388.6	All Right
5,544.6	Rain to Fuckin' Rain
5,702.6	Blue Sky
5,894.3	Fine
6,025.3	Cloudy
6,164.7	Rain to Fine
6,309.7	Fine
6,456.2	Jesus, Windy
6,611.5	Rain, Rain, Rain
6,774.1	Fine, Fine
6,899.5	OK
7,044.5	OK
7,209.1	Cloudy to Fine
7,355.2	OK
7,487.0	Windy
7,628.7	Very Fine!
7,778.3	Completely Blue Sky
7,915.8	Rain to Hot
8,066.9	OK to Rain
8,186.2	Beautiful Sky
8,345.5	Rain to Fine
8,503.7	Cloudy
8,639.7	Superb!
8,791.6	Fine
8,924.7	Fine, Fine
9,077.4	Cloudy to Sun!
9,233.3	Lovely!Lovely!!
9,392.6	Cloudy...
9,528.6	Fuckin' Rain!
9,665.7	Rain and better
9,796.0	Fine
9,826.2	Superb!
9,831.4	Fine
9,887.7	Very Fine
9,971.8	Beautiful

Date	Location	Day Distance (km)
Aug-07	Horn - Mem	78.4
Aug-08	Mem - Gusum	52.1
Aug-09	Gusum - Gamleby	68.4
Aug-10	Gamleby - Langstroempe	85.0
Aug-11	Langstroempe - Aseda	87.8
Aug-12	Aseda - Torne	86.3
Aug-13	Torne - Hostveda	88.8
Aug-14	Hostveda - Copenhagen	122.4
Aug-18	Copenhagen - Vordingborg	115.0
Aug-19	Vordingborg - Zedano	125.7
Aug-20	Zedano - Hamburg	137.3
Aug-21	Hamburg - Sottrum	100.0
Aug-22	Sottrumn - Wildeshausen	91.9
Aug-23	Wildeshausen - Border(Holland side)	135.7
Aug-24	Border(Holland side) - Nieuw-Milligen	109.9
Aug-25	Nieuw-Milligen - Amsterdam	81.3
Aug-27	Amsterdam - Moerdijk	122.6
Aug-28	Moerdijk - Bruxelles	131.0
Aug-30	Bruxelles -Oostende	164.9
Aug-31	Oostende - Dover	112.7
Sep-01	Dover - Maidstone	81.9
Sep-02	Maidstone - London	91.6
Sep-04	London - Hook Norton	142.9
Sep-06	Hook Norton - around Newwent	79.5
Sep-07	around Newwent - Brecon	106.7
Sep-08	Brecon - Carmarthen	87.9
Sep-09	Carmarthen - Rosslare	89.9
Sep-10	Rosslare - Greystones	146.4
Sep-11	**Greystones - St.James Gate, Dublin**	**39.4**

Total Distance (km	Weather
10,050.2	Cloudy
10,102.3	Cloudy
10,170.7	Just Fine
10,255.7	Blue Sky
10,343.5	Sun
10,429.8	Lovely
10,518.6	Slightly rain to Sun
10,641.0	Cloudy to Sun!
10,756.0	OK
10,881.7	Windy
11,019.0	**Windy**
11,119.0	Fuckin' Rain
11,210.9	All Right
11,346.6	Windy but slight sun
11,456.5	Windy, Rain, Cold
11,537.8	better
11,660.4	Windy but sunny
11,791.4	So so
11,956.3	Slight rain to cloudy
12,069.0	Sunny
12,150.9	Lovely to OK
12,242.5	Not so good
12,385.4	OK
12,464.9	Cloudy
12,571.6	Sun to Rain
12,659.5	Rain
12,749.4	Windy to Rain to Lovely
12,895.8	Cloudy but Superb
12,935.2	**Fuckin' Lovely**